PRACTICAL PAGANISM

PRACTICAL PAGANISM

ANTHONY KEMP AND J.M. SERTORI

ROBERT HALE · LONDON

Typeset by
Derek Doyle and Associates, Mold.
Printed in Great Britain by
St Edmundsbury Press Limited, Bury St Edmunds
and bound by
WBC Book Manufacturers Limited, Bridgend

Acknowledgements

There is no such thing as a ready-packaged Pagan and all of us who tread the Path owe an immense debt to others who have accompanied us, both as teachers and companions. I have been fortunate in that I have been privileged to study and share experiences with a wide variety of loving friends over the years, and as a result have been able to pass on some of my ideas to others.

First there was Debbie, a true priestess, who taught me the ways of the wise as well as some necessary lessons about materialism, together with her partner and fellow Child of the Sun, Sir Bard. Secondly, Doreen Valiente, whose books provided me with a common-sense framework for practical knowledge in the early days, and specifically for the Coven Charge on page 199. Other authors who have influenced me include Vivianne Crowley, Marion Green and Murry Hope.

Then there are the true friends with whom I have danced the spiral dance from time to time, or with whom I have discussed the meaning of it all: Alison; Rainbow Jo, priestess and mother; Fee; Morag and her coven, Jin, Sara and Kate; the Lady Olivia Durdin Robertson and her late brother; Sara Robinson who ordained me; Phil of the wild places; Vivienne; Karina who has passed on to the Summerlands; Willow; Ayla who tolerated my love affair with a word processor; Kate who asked the right questions; and Corinne, the first French initiate. There are also the Children of the Goddess, Kirsty, Tobias, Sebbie and Gemma. Lastly, and certainly by no means the least, the Lady Romayne, robe-maker extraordinary and a fount of common sense.

I also owe a debt of gratitude to members of the Rainbow Tribe and the Convoy, who helped mould my opinions, as well as to the current environmental protest groups such as Dragon and the Dongas, whose activities for a better world are showing a way forward.

A.K.

Thanks to Charlotte and Chelsey (secret agents) for all their work on this project, Jane Struthers for tarot trivia, and to Kate for putting up with the ceaseless typing. Simon Tomlin and Michael Bennie ploughed through the final draft with an editorial *athame*, though any remaining mistakes are my responsibility.

J.S.

Contents

Illustrations

Credits

Anthony Kemp: 1–8. Doreen Valiente: 9.

Introduction

Pagan ideas took root in Britain in the 1960s with the reinvention of witchcraft, and rapidly spread to the United States and Australasia. Initially secretive, Wicca became more open with the publication of a number of important books in the early 1980s. Since then, there has been a massive change of emphasis which has largely gone unnoticed in publications on the subject.

Today, there is a far more eclectic approach to what has become the fastest-growing spiritual movement or religion in Britain. This has been echoed by other developments in other countries, notably the newly liberated Eastern European and Baltic States. The membership of the Pagan Federation, the body that links all the disparate traditions, has doubled annually over the last few years, as more and more people seek to discover a new spiritual dimension for themselves.

The essential aim of this book is to provide readers with a practical, step-by-step introduction to Pagan ideas and practices, which they can try for themselves without having to 'join' anyone else's coven or organization. The authors do not seek to convert, but merely to present some novel ideas for readers to consider. In this regard, we have approached our work from two different directions. Kemp uses a phenomenological approach, looking out at the world from inside Paganism, seeking to answer the many questions he has been asked by new Pagans in recent years. These questions often take the same form, or make the same assumptions, and hopefully this book will save time and effort, or at least encourage fruitful debate among new Pagans. Part of Kemp's answer comes in the form of suggested rituals, in an attempt to develop a revised Pagan liturgy for the use of all denominations.

Sertori's approach is theological; it is an attempt to take all the contradictory traditions of Paganism and hammer them into a coherent whole, to find a common ground upon which all Pagans can happily stand together in a unified tradition. Many Pagan books are self-defeating because of their dogmatic reliance on sources now known to be untrustworthy. Our book aims to show the underlying truth beneath the disparate traditions, and encourage Pagans to accept each other, and their own weaknesses.

Read on, in perfect love and perfect trust.

1 Paganism: The New Age Religion

Say you are a Pagan and you will get strange looks. People will edge away from you almost imperceptibly, eyes darting behind you in search of a black cat or a broomstick. Their speech will suddenly become more measured and careful, as they try not to anger you and incur your spell-casting wrath. Is that when you know you have really arrived as a Pagan?

Alternatively you may be accused of Satanism and told you are going to go straight to hell. You will be cut off, cast out and told never to darken your friend's door again. A lifetime of persecution and misunderstanding awaits. Is this what Paganism means?

You may also watch with amazement as members of the opposite sex start to gravitate in your direction. Suddenly you find yourself the centre of attention at parties, and pretty young things keep on asking you if it is true about all those orgies and all those naked dances under the moon. Suddenly you have become dark and mysterious, an exotic, erotic stranger they just *have* to get to know better. Is this what it is like to be a Pagan?

Let us get a few facts straight. A Pagan is not a witch, although most witches are Pagan. Witchcraft (or Wicca) is just part of Paganism, as Protestantism is just part of Christianity. Yes, witches can cast spells. No, they will not try and turn you into a frog. Yes, a lot of them are women. No, they are not all ancient, toothless hags. You may be surprised to know that some witches also work as fashion models.

A Pagan is not a Satanist. You have to be a Christian before you can believe in Satan, and Pagans are not Christians. Pagans, like Christians, refuse to harm other people, be they Pagan or not. Their religion emphasizes the positive, the natural and the nurturing; none of these things exist in the sick perversion that is Satanism. Pagans are not evil, Pagans

13

do not seek to harm others, Pagans are not the enemies of Christianity, although many Christians have confused Satanism and Paganism and tarred them with the same brush.

A Pagan is not an orgiastic loon, cavorting with a coven of sex-kittens beneath a cloudless, starry sky. It is true that Pagans are less prudish than many of their Christian counterparts, but this is because Paganism has no concept of sin in the Christian sense. The Pagan universe is divided into male and female principles, eternally balanced, eternally loving and eternally in need of each other. For this reason, a sacred marriage between a man and a woman is one of the highest forms of Pagan ritual, and the sexual act itself is a symbol of the creative act that began the universe. A Pagan husband and wife are encouraged to celebrate the beauty of their union in bed as well as out of it, but this is normally as far as it goes. Nuns who are 'married to Christ' are not expected to take the son of God off on a honeymoon, and Pagans are not expected to swap partners, commit strange sexual acts or otherwise indulge in weird behaviour. What really annoys their persecutors, however, is that unlike Christians, Pagans are perfectly at liberty to do these things if they want to, and there is no 'payback', no sin. Many alleged Pagan heresies only exist in the minds of their persecutors, who have subliminally mapped their own fantasies on to someone else, rather than admit to their preacher that it is they who really want to do the deeds. Repression breeds some terrible things, but there is no repression in Paganism. And yet, merely because there is no repression, it does not necessarily follow that there is a tradition of unbridled libertinism. All things in moderation, including sex.

The Origins of Paganism

This is a book about modern Paganism, or neo-Paganism. It is not a collection of fairy stories about the gods and goddesses of the ancient Europeans, nor is it a vague collection of spells and cantrips requiring eyes of newts and toes of bats. Paganism has been around for centuries, and has undergone many changes, and modern Pagans are interested in those elements that have endured across the many boundaries of geography and time, not those which have varied wildly from village to village and tribe to tribe.

Different races worship different pantheons of deities, but the same groups turn up in culture after culture. Carl Jung called them archetypes, Pagans call them gods and goddesses, each of them with a character that reflects some aspect of our own humanity. Different races have different festivals, but the same cycles turn up in culture after culture. The year itself is a celebration, a festival of birth and death in tune with the seasons as witnessed by pastoral communities: the sowing of the seeds and the harvesting of the crops. Pagans, too, celebrate this eternal wheel of change, recognizing that all living things are born, grow old and die, returning once more to the Earth that spawned them.

Different races and religious traditions have different laws. Pagans have very, very few indeed, which is why Paganism has often remained buried beneath other religious traditions. There is no law that says a Pagan cannot be a Christian as well, or a Muslim or a Jew. Some American witches are also pastors in regional churches. It is the current Japanese fashion to be born Shinto (Pagan), marry Christian and die a Buddhist; all these traditions are mixed and matched, depending on the desires of the individual not the organization. Paganism does not have a headquarters, a pontiff issuing orders or a nerve centre making the rules. Paganism is about what you want from your spiritual life. Nobody can tell you what to do, and nobody but yourself can punish you for your mistakes. Paganism is all about being your own spiritual boss, although there are some people who would rather be led around like sheep.

The name itself has had a chequered past. The word *paganus* was originally used in Latin to mean 'countrified' or 'rural', and became a common derogatory term in the Roman army for hicks and yokels. A commission in the army was one of the few ways of obtaining citizenship, and so anyone out in the country would be a *paganus* for as long as he did not join up. Over time, the word came to mean a non-soldier. When the Christians arrived on the scene, many called themselves *militia Christi* (soldiers of Christ), and with this introduction of martial terminology, some began referring to non-Christians as civvies, or *pagani*.

So even from the early days, the term 'pagan' has been quite vague. As far as Christians are concerned, it is very simple – if you are not a Christian, you are a Pagan. A *History of Paganism* would be as unwritable and irrelevant as an *Atlas of Infidels* (the world minus the Muslims), or a *History of the Gentiles* (the world minus the Jews).

Born of particular places and times, modern Paganism has been constructed from what little we have been able to salvage of the beliefs of our ancestors before they were made Christians by default. There is no rationale in the Bible for Christmas, Easter or Hallowe'en, no talk of saints or purgatory. These are all Pagan ideas, torn from Latin and Greek poems, adapted from local festivals to ancient gods, held at the same times of the year to ensure that the locals could continue with their regular parties and festivities. Even today, how many people outside the fundamentalist fringe, are really, truly Christian? How many British families do not go to church, but nevertheless pay lip-service to the incredibly un-Christian festival of Christmas? Moreover, we know that Jesus was not even born in December. How many Catholics truly believe that the Pope is infallible, and follow his every whim and encyclical? Indeed, how many priests do?

Paganism recognizes that Christianity has achieved great success, but also that many supposedly Christian ideas were purloined from other traditions. The easy way in which the Christians wrote off and dismissed the many indigenous religious traditions of Europe hides some important omissions. They would have us believe that the Romans were impressed with their beliefs, and that the Emperor Constantine converted, followed by the rest of his empire. Constantine did convert, but only on his deathbed, a last-minute insurance policy that hardly suggests a real commitment. The rest of his empire was hardly crazy about it either. Although there were Christian churches and a nominal rule of Christianity, life still went on as before. At a local level, the common people were more bothered by their feudal lords than by the pronouncements of the Pope. Supposedly pious deeds such as the Crusades seemed to have more to do with plunder and booty than 'rescuing the Holy Land'.

To draw a flippant analogy, the history of Christianity has worked in much the same way as Disney cartoons. A central authority collated and adapted the myths and legends of many disparate cultures, turning them into their own unique tales. Just as most children today think of Cinderella, Robin Hood and the Little Mermaid as Disney productions, with little knowledge of their original versions, Christianity too co-opted many Pagan aspects and claimed them as its own. Some Pagan gods reappeared as Christian saints. The Pagan cult of the Mother Goddess was reborn as the worship of the Virgin Mary, although of course she was now regarded as the inferior of the supposedly male God Almighty. Pagans, ever accepting and willing to take the path of least resistance, happily allowed the Christians to build their churches and preach their gospels of love and forgiveness, but they did not expect the ethics of 'loving thy neighbour' to degenerate over time into intolerance and persecution.

Europe did not in fact immediately become Christian when the people were told to do so. Many paid lip service to the Christian ideology, but it was not as deeply ingrained as many assume. For many centuries, the Christian mass was conducted in Latin, a language incomprehensible to the common people, and to all intents and purposes, Europe remained primarily Pagan, but with a Christian ruling class at the top of the hierarchy. Because Paganism was rarely written down (most scholars, of course, being Christian monks), there are few records of exactly what was done and where, but the cycle of the seasons and the passing of the generations eventually ingrained several recurring festivals and attitudes in the Pagan world. Christianity has incorporated these too, but this book is about the many aspects of Paganism which Christianity has ignored. The dangerous, deadly teachings that men and women are equal, that a woman's creative power should be celebrated and not shut away, that man is not the most superior creature in the universe, but part of a living, breathing entity that is planet Earth – all these things are part of Paganism.

In these more enlightened times, we are still only beginning to unravel the many traditions hidden within the Christian church as it grew and flourished. Modern Pagans believe that much was lost when this Middle Eastern pastoral religion, which saw human beings as sheep and their priests as noble shepherds, was imposed for political reasons upon an entire continent, and then on the world. Modern-day Pagans want to retain the positive and beneficial elements of Christianity. But they also want to disestablish the many contradictions within the Christian philosophy – that we should not kill, but can fight in holy wars, that humanity is being punished for an 'original sin', that the world will end in a terrifying conflict and only the faithful (or the generous) will be saved.

The New Testament did not spring into the world fully formed, but expanded and contracted as whims and trends brought books into and out of favour. It was only eventually finalized several centuries after the birth of Christ, at a council of churchmen who determined the final contents by vote. Some books just made it in, others were just squeezed out. The homogeneous, righteous face that Christianity presents to the world was only decided after many bitter disputes. Are religious icons graven images? Should priests marry? Should there be women priests? Are good and evil equal forces? Is there a hell? Is Mohammed a prophet? Should priests have beards, even? All these questions combined to form the differing religious traditions of the Western world, but at a grass

roots level, popular superstitions remained unchanged. Churches were
built over many Pagan sacred sites. Many Pagan priests became adherents of Christianity, intrigued by its new perspective on the divine.

It is only now, in the wake of the 1960s and after several decades of
false starts, that Paganism is achieving its rightful place as a recognized,
informed religion. These are the days of the Pagan New Testament, and
it is still being written. This book may become part of its tradition, or it
may not; that is for you, not the authors, to decide.

Witchery and Sorcery

Most Pagan books tell you about the various pantheons of Europe. They
will describe indigenous religions, and tell fairy stories about the gods
and goddesses of the Norsemen, the Germans and the Celts. The problem with that is that it implies an unbroken tradition from ancient times
to the present day, and that simply is not the case. Modern Paganism is
truly modern; even its earliest beginnings cannot be traced back further
than the eighteenth century. There have always been elements of Pagan,
non-Christian ideologies buried beneath the surface of Christianity, but
that does not necessarily mean that there has been an unchanging tradition of 'secret' knowledge for the last 2,000 years. Some people did
maintain a close contact with the spirit world and the paranormal; in
some areas they became great priests and saints of the Christian church,
in others they were persecuted for 'witchcraft', in still others, they
became early doctors and scientists, healers and philosophers. In
general, however, most Pagan traditions are extremely recent inventions,
although they may draw on ideas and accoutrements that have been in
existence for thousands of years. The shamanistic tradition has been part
of the human spirit for millennia, but modern-day shamans owe their
existence more to the American Indian tradition and the psychedelic
1960s than to mystics from a thousand years in the past. The only
exception is the Druidic tradition, which can be traced back a couple of
centuries. But Druidry was a perfectly acceptable pastime for Christians
in the eighteenth and nineteenth centuries, and the relationship of those
people to the historical Druids is tenuous.

Wicca (the tradition of 'witchcraft') has provided the greatest problem
for historians of Paganism. Its practitioners in the early twentieth
century claimed to be the inheritors of an ancient religion, pointing to
the historical 'witch trials' as evidence of the persecution of their philo-

sophical ancestors. But much of the evidence of their tradition appears to die out the further back we go – there is little evidence of Wicca before the first half of the twentieth century, and less still if we subscribe to the current thinking that the so-called 'witch trials' persecuted few, if any, real witches. There are, of course, still those who point to the circular nature of the argument: if witches were persecuted they would not want to leave any tracks; if they left no traces, there would be no evidence; therefore if we cannot find evidence of real witches between, say, the seventeenth century and the 1940s, that itself is a kind of proof that they *did* exist! Such para-logic has often been used to explain the lack of evidence, and also the many inconsistencies in differing covens – the garbled information is the result of centuries spent 'underground'. We should not expect to find written records of witchery, say the apologists, because any eighteenth-century witch stupid enough to write down her spells, magical workings and coven membership, could not possibly have been the genuine article. Such specious arguments have done serious witchcraft no favours at all.

Pagans acknowledge that there is such a thing as magic, but say that it need not be sanitized by the empty rituals of the Christian church. Undoubtedly, people in different places at different points in history have developed powers they could not quite understand. A knowledge of herbalism, an understanding of acupuncture, a certain ability to sense the paranormal, perhaps even clairvoyance and clairaudience, all these things are magical powers that modern witches try to hone and improve. A belief in the old gods, be it as genuine deities or as symbolic representations of the archetypes and elements of the human characters, is also a sign of traditional 'witchery', but that term would have been applied to anyone who dared to question a single element of the Christian tradition. Such people have undoubtedly existed throughout history, in considerable numbers, but they are not necessarily the precursors of Paganism. They worked singly or in small, temporary groups. They were separated by history and geography, and their many disparate Pagan ideologies died with them. The same 'discoveries' were made over and over again, and then lost once more. Only a few ceremonies and festivals have survived, incorporated into the Christian tradition or one of the many 'secret societies' that sprang up during the Industrial Revolution.

People need ceremony. It helps affirm who they are and makes them feel like part of a group. It also spurs them on and concentrates their minds. The 'secretive ceremonial' of Freemasonry and Rosicrucianism had their mirrors in many friendly societies, designed as grass-roots banks and insurance companies in the days before building societies and trade unions. But none of these strands really helps explain why there has been a sudden resurgence of interest in Paganism. Our interest in a simpler time, before Christian persecution and hypocrisy, also owes something to the ecology movement, both current and historical.

Ecology

The historical ecology movement was not so much a philosophy as a state of utter shock. Environmental change was normally too slow to spot; the Saxons hardly considered that they would eventually cut down all the trees in such a huge forest, or that the peat they were digging for in Norfolk would leave huge holes that would eventually fill to become lakes. Life was so short, technology so inefficient and the demands of the population so light, that man's farming, hunting and building were rarely noted for the damage being done to the environment. There are scattered references here and there, mainly in times of war, to instances of environmental loss – the Greeks felling all the trees on a single island to repair their ships, or the burning and looting that accompanied the fall of a castle or city – but generally ecological change was too slow to be noticed by a single generation.

All that changed in the nineteenth century, when the Industrial Revolution brought sweeping changes that altered the landscape for ever. In 1810, 80 per cent of the population of the United Kingdom lived in the countryside. By 1910, 80 per cent lived in cities. For the first time in history, the world was changing so fast that people could witness it happening around them. Cartoons of the day depicted wheezing traction engines chewing up arable land and covering it with smokestacks and red bricks. Some people became concerned about change for change's sake, and some began to hark back to the 'good old days' of pastoral bliss. An interest in medieval times, or even further back, in the supposedly carefree life of the Greeks and Romans, fostered a related interest in the gods and beliefs of these bygone ages.

The truly modern (some might argue post modern) Pagan movement owes much to this attitude among our close ancestors, but it also owes much to the Green ideas of the 1960s. Fearful of nuclear power and concerned about pollution, the baby-boom generation that reached maturity in the 1960s began to concern itself with Mother Earth. The emphasis on non-traditional philosophies and the *de facto* Shamanism encouraged by the drug culture helped to bring about a state of mind that was more accepting of new ideas. The clincher, in many ways, was the space programme, which hurtled men into orbit and sent us back one of the most valuable photographs ever taken: the blue-green Earth, shining in space like a jewel.

For the first time, people could actually look and see their world in space – a fragile, insignificant cradle for the human race but a single, definable entity. If nothing else created a concern for ecology and helped to foster the concept of a united, loving Earth with mankind in co-operation and harmony, it was this single stunning vision of our planet from the outside.

Christians saw it as proof of the existence of God and the creation. Scientists saw it as proof of their theories of cosmology and geology. The people who were to become the Pagans of the New Age just saw it, and marvelled at its beauty. A major factor in modern Paganism has been the desire to keep it beautiful. Mankind only has one nest, and the Gaia that gave birth to us should be cared for lest she rejects us.

Books and the Pagan 'Revival'

Books have always played an important part in the history of Paganism. Their earliest influence was negative – because of the absence of literacy and a literature, many elements of ancient Paganism were lost or misinterpreted. Books are important symbols of learning, all the more so in the ancient world, where the ability to read marked someone out as a strange demigod with magical powers – someone who could draw on the memories of others long dead, and seek help from authorities he or she had never met. The Christian religion has always presented a very contradictory attitude towards learning. Its own holy book is called, in Greek, simply 'The Book' (*Biblos*). You only need the one Bible, such terminology seems to say: forsake all others. If something is not in it, it is not allowed. So throw away your Koran, your Talmud, and your *Tao Te Ching*, look not for understanding in works of science. The Bible is the only book you should ever need, and if you disagree there must be something truly, badly wrong with you. During the witch trials, many intellectuals were undoubtedly wrongfully persecuted simply for owning reading matter which was inappropriate in the eyes of the Church. Wisdom of an unsanctioned nature was always treated with suspicion, and ignorance of its uses may have sentenced many a herbalist, philosopher, inventor or writer to an untimely and undeserved death.

In the modern age, books have come to play a different role in the history of Paganism, as several factors united to create a proto-Pagan literature. In 1899 Charles Leland's *Aradia* was published. This tale of Italian sorcery, supposedly describing one branch of a large coven of European witches, was notable in Britain in that it introduced the concept of a Goddess-oriented religion that challenged the male-dominated religion of the last two millennia. It eventually proved to be a great influence on modern Paganism, especially the Gardnerian Wiccan field, which lifted large sections of its ideas.

Leland himself was inspired by another book, which was published in French in 1862 but was not available in Britain until five years after *Aradia*. Jules Michelet's *La Sorcière* was published in English in 1904. Michelet, an avowed republican and a staunch anti-Catholic, crafted this literary pot-boiler from scattered Renaissance pamphlets, anti-Church propaganda and his own uninformed imaginings of life in the Middle Ages. He imagined a secret Pagan religion that had preserved all that was noble and good about our ancient ancestors throughout the Dark Ages and the predations of the Church. In his desire to tell a good story and present an intriguing alternative, he turned every preconception on its head. He suggested a female clergy, a love of nature instead of progress and a true, binding commandment of peace and love. It was this, claimed Michelet, that had eventually bubbled through after years of repression to create the Enlightenment. The Reformation and Renaissance, and by association, his beloved French Revolution, were the direct results of this ancient wisdom finally leaving its secretive keepers and finding the ears, hearts and minds of those in positions of power and authority.

The fictional and semi-fictional idea of a female or male–female religion gained greater credibility in 1933, when the archaeologist and folklorist Margaret Murray published *The God of the Witches*. Murray argued that the many persecutions, rumours and folk tales of witchcraft and sorcery over the centuries were the vestigial remnants of a once-great native European tradition, now almost completely lost. Although her work has since been discredited because of her over-selective treatment of her sources, at the time it was a vital contributor to the Pagan tradition.

Basing their ideas on the writings of Murray, Leland and Michelet, drawing on anthropological theses such as J.G. Frazer's *Golden Bough* and the traditions of secret societies such as Freemasonry, people began to 'revive' what they saw as their rightful, ancestral religion.

The Dawn of a New Age

All the above factors prepared the ground for modern Paganism. None of them is the one vital, crucial influence because modern Paganism is a truly modern phenomenon. False memories of an ancestral past, true knowledge of traditional worship and belief, self-awareness and ecological interests all help to encourage a sense of Pagan understanding, but it is only in this time of lessening persecution and the free dissemination of information that Paganism can really flourish. Witches or proto-witches are no longer hunted down for daring to suggest that women can be priests, or for researching the powers of the human mind; as they flourish and their network of friends extend, their experiences are recorded for others to draw upon, not lost for eternity as has happened to so many of their predecessors.

Modern Paganism is still in its infancy. It has progressed over many years through trial and error, and still faces many challenges. It is only recently that it has had to deal with the concept of death and funereal rites as its founding generation ages, or theorize about the concepts of marriage and divorce, or decide upon the ethics of bringing up children in a Pagan tradition, when that tradition itself decrees that all members should attend of their own free will. This book is an attempt to rationalize some of the many competing and contradictory strands of modern Paganism, to encourage discourse as we stand on the brink of the New Age, and offer suggestions for the next steps Pagans should consider taking.

2   What Do Pagans Believe?

There is no Pagan manual that makes an incontrovertible, infallible statement of 'the Truth', footnoted to the effect that anyone who disagrees cannot be a Pagan. For example, the Pagan gods are regarded by some as real and by some as symbolic, but this difference of view does not really matter. However, a survey of any cross-section of Pagan groups will reveal a number of recurring theories.

Most Pagans have one single fundamental law, a prime directive that is valued above all others. It is: 'If it harm none, do as you will.' This commandment, or slight rephrasings of it, is the most common principle in Pagan religions. Originating in the Wiccan Witch's Rede (Law), it has been adopted by many other sectors of Paganism, not as a religious maxim, but as a general guideline for living. It also bears an uncanny resemblance to the Christian maxim, 'Do unto others as you would be done by', a hearty reminder that Christianity was an inclusive liberal-minded religion in its early days, before it became convinced of its infallibility and mandate to proselytize.

Modern Paganism has many similarities with early Christianity, and modern Pagans hope to keep the good and discard the bad of the beliefs of that era. The Faith of the early Christians was a reaction to the beliefs of the Old Testament; Jesus was an anarchist figure in the eyes of the established Temple, and committed the unforgivable crime of teaching that love for one another was of paramount importance. Early Christians, too, were a minority group persecuted for their beliefs, with several contradictory traditions.

The manner in which these contradictions were ironed out, however, served to create more problems for Christianity. Eventually, a central authority issued proclamations on the nature of good and bad teachings, the acceptable and unacceptable books of the Bible and the right or wrong way to be a Christian. An infallible hierarchy was established, and human beings (fallible creatures all!) set the rules in stone, so that only an act of heresy could change the nature of the Church. Pagans, on the other hand, recognize that the future will bring changes to their religion. We hope to learn from the mistakes of the early Christian Church, and not to repeat too many of them. We also hope to become friends with the Christian movement, since there are too many similarities between our beliefs for us to ignore each other. Throughout history, Pagans have been persecuted, both for being 'ignorant' unbelievers and for more sinister reasons. The dogmatic insistence on the right of the Bible's interpreters to decide how others should live has nothing to do with the word of a loving divine being. It has grown out of the earthly concerns of human beings who have forgotten the spirit of their religion. The only modern-day antagonism that may be felt by Pagans towards Christianity, or indeed any other hierarchical religion, is in its insistence that it is the *only* way to worship, and that other ways should be eradicated.

This view is particularly amusing to Pagans, since we are fully aware how many supposedly Christian practices are thinly disguised Pagan rituals. The Christian pantheon of saints, the 'household gods' of the Nativity and, in southern Europe, of patron saints, the customs of Christmas and Easter, and indeed the way in which the life of Christ has been turned into a seasonal cycle of festivals, are all rooted deeply within the tradition of Paganism. Despite the pronouncements of the Church and its fatuous conviction that it is the one true faith, throughout history it has continually drifted towards Pagan traditions. This is partly because the 'conquered' peoples who converted to Christianity had their own local traditions, which the Church saw as a threat to its power.

Science has placed an unbearable strain on the supposedly incontrovertible words of the Bible. Much of it has been shown to be a historically and scientifically inaccurate account of events in a small area of the Middle East, self-contradictory and increasingly irrelevant in the modern age. That is not to say for a moment that it does not contain words of wisdom, just that the most open-minded Christians are forced to regard it more and more as well-intentioned stories from an ancient sect of Judaism rather than literal truth. The moment an individual admits that the entire story of the creation might not be contained in Genesis, that the six days of God's work, for example, are allegorical rather than literal, they are conceding that there is more to the world than the outmoded explanations offered by the Bible, and they are already on the way to accepting other faiths as part of life. In earlier times, they could be burned as witches for daring to think in such a way.

According to the fundamentalist rules of the Church, anyone who disbelieves a part of the Bible, be it the literal parting of the Red Sea or the Virgin birth, is a Pagan by default.

No Easy Answers

All philosophies are ways of explaining the world. Whether they are sciences or religions, ultimately they involve a faith in their power to explain all that needs to be explained. They all have their own ways of divination. But whether they involve prayer, runes and tarot cards, or psychoanalysis and statistics, they are all merely inadequate attempts to fathom the unfathomable, to come up with a way of explaining the entire universe. Yet no belief system can encompass everything, although all of them contain elements of the truth. In this way, Paganism is closer to a science than a religion, because it is happy to acknowledge that there are some things it cannot explain. Unlike most religions, it does not offer easy answers, or a set of rewards and punishments to make people feel better about themselves and their problems.

The commonest questions asked by newcomers interested in Paganism are usually those that will be familiar to anyone who has been a member of an organized religion. Religions need hooks to bring in new customers, and some will offer whatever it takes. Many people want reassurance about eternal life, the opportunity to be saved from guilt, or a licence to commit new sins with a 'get out of jail free' card. Yes, the Christian priest will say, there is life after death. That is because God made the universe and he loves you, and as long as you do as I say, the creator of the universe will look after you until you die, and then you'll live in a holiday resort called Heaven, populated by loads of people like me.

The Pagan view is rather different. Pagans do not really know if there is life after death, because this is not a point that all traditions agree on. The Pagan answer is that it does not matter. If your soul departs your body and goes on to different things after your death, then that is good news for those you leave behind, and for you. If the afterlife is improved in direct relation to this life, then so much the better, it is a good idea to be nice to people and to strive to be a good person. If there is reincarnation, the same applies. But if there is no life after death, if this threescore years and ten is all we have, then surely it is sensible to make the most of it. The Pagan policy of harming no one will produce the same results whatever the believer's standing on the afterlife. Pagans do not need to be kept in line with vague threats about Hell. They strive to be good people because goodness is part of their rules for living.

Most Pagans would like to believe in life after death, and many of us do, but we do not use it as a mental crutch or as a means of bending others to our will. We do not go to empty churches and mutter into the dark to assuage our guilty feelings about those we have lost; we do not shut the stable door after the horse has bolted. We strive to show our loved ones how we feel when they are still alive to appreciate it. As for our own souls, we will find out soon enough whether they live on after we die. There is no hurry, but in the meantime let us love one another and do good. There are Pagan funeral rites (see Chapter 11) that mark the passing of those we hold dear, but let us be honest, the rituals are for the benefit of the living.

Gods and Goddesses

A similar indifference is found in the Pagan philosophy of gods and goddesses. Most Pagan traditions have divine figures as objects of worship and reverence. These can range from the Dianic single Goddess (a deliberate reaction to Christianity's insistence on a single male God) to entire families of deities. Pagans believe that one of the ways in which our ancestors understood the subconscious and the human psyche was through archetypes which were often given personalities through art and sculpture. Gods of war, love, motherhood, fertility etc helped believers to focus their minds and concentrate on their needs and desires, and different races developed their own, surprisingly similar, traditions. There are Pagan organizations that revere the gods and goddesses of Greece, Rome, Scandinavia, India, China, Japan and several Native American tribes, as well as ancient Germanic deities and many, many Celtic divinities. In Europe and white North America, the Celtic and Norse traditions are particularly well represented, because many Europeans feel that these divinities – their ways, characters, stories and trials – somehow speak to something within our souls. Call it race memory, call it DNA, there is something about these particular archetypes that fires our imagination, stirs our passions and spurs us on to greater efforts. When we worship them, we are really worshipping their aspects as revealed in ourselves.

For Pagans, the most important aspect of our belief is the eternal union of male and female, the two generative forces in the natural world that exist to create life, and with it happiness. Pagans understand that there is a creative power in the universe, and celebrate it through the polarity of male and female. We value both sides of this polarity, and reject the notion that one gender is 'better' than the other. We celebrate the differences between men and women, and involve both genders in our religious practices. The universe is composed of male and female principles, and so is our religious understanding of it. Many Pagans worship gods and goddesses as the embodiment of natural forces. Others will acknowledge the rituals of worship as a ceremony of integrating the human community, without necessarily agreeing that the gods and goddesses are real. Pantheons of archetypical deities are found throughout the world; Pagans do not recognize one pantheon above all others, but acknowledge that all religions are culturally and geographically defined attempts to explain the universe. Since religions the world over are all very similar, they must all have a grain of truth within them, and must be respected and tolerated.

Respect for the Natural (and Supernatural) World

Paganism acknowledges that humans are occupants of planet Earth, but not its masters. The universe was not created for our benefit, we are part of it, not the reason for its existence. There is room within Paganism for the theory of evolution, since whether we were created as we are by the fiat of an almighty God, or evolved over millions of years from primitive organisms, the end result is the same: our intelligence sets us apart from the other creatures of the Earth, not as 'superior' beings, but as beings with a particular responsibility to look after the environment that produced us. All Pagans strive to live in harmony with the natural world, many support the Green movement or ecological groups of some description. We do not necessarily regard the modern world as evil, but acknowledge that some of our acts may not be to the benefit of future generations. To steal another quote from the Bible, men come and go, but the Earth abides. The Earth does not 'mind' what we do, since it will endure long after we have wiped ourselves off its face. The ecological movement is in fact an entity of self-preservation, to ensure that we as a species last longer by living responsibly. The life of the world around us is a beautiful thing, an eternal poem to the beauty of Nature and the connectedness of all things. Pagans would like to keep things that way, not bend Nature to their will. We are part of this planet and would like to stay part of it.

Pagans acknowledge that there is some force in the universe greater than human beings. Others may call it the supernatural or the paranormal, but an essential tenet of Pagan belief is that it is the exact opposite. It is both natural and normal, the only thing that makes it 'super' or 'para' is our own inadequate understanding. There is a natural potential within us all to outdo the puny physical limitations of our bodies. Pagans also believe that this power can be harnessed within ourselves. In effect, we believe in magic – real magic – and believe that we have the power within us to achieve any goal we set ourselves. Everyone in the world is a little miracle, and human beings never cease to impress each other with their powers of endurance or efforts of will. In order to distinguish Pagans' use of paranormal energies from the modern-day efforts of conjurors, charlatans and children's entertainers, many Pagans will use the term 'magick'. The spelling is a deliberate attempt to distance what we do in all seriousness from the 'eye of newt and toe of bat' of popular mythology.

Faith in Magic and Human Potential

Magic in the Pagan sense is not the spell-casting, lightning-throwing wizardry of Hollywood films. In fact, Pagan magic is about the transformation of the self. It is more concerned with creative visualization and with concentrating the mind than it is with turning people into frogs and sneaking love potions into people's drinks. Pagans accept that magic is real (that the paranormal is part of the normal), but also that the use of rituals and ceremonies helps to concentrate the mind. Even many atheists today like to get married in church. Why? Because the ritual and the ceremony has a meaning for them. The effort, the expense, the stress, the dressing-up, the many customs and traditions, all combine to make a wedding day a special day. They could simply pop into the register office on their way to the supermarket, but even today many still prefer to remind themselves of the importance of the vows they are taking.

Pagan magical rituals work in a similar way. We do not understand the powers of the human mind or the links and influences that bind us to the natural world, but we do know that there are ways we can access the world beyond. Cultures throughout history have used rituals to bring themselves closer to the so-called paranormal: the drugs and drumming of the American Indians, the incense and theatre of the Catholic church, the ceremonial warding-off of evil in feng shui, each is merely another way of focusing the human mind on the job at hand. More often than not, the job at hand is an aspiration or a desire, perhaps a question, and whether it is achieved by prayer or psychoanalysis is immaterial.

A Pagan might discover the answer to something in tarot cards, believe that they are meaningless but that the apparent pattern to their reading jogs something that is niggling at the subconscious. Have the cards spoken, or has the Pagan's mind really just realized something that it knew all along? Ultimately, it does not matter; what matters is that it has worked. Pagans do not seek to prove or disprove the vagaries of astrology, tarot cards, runes, the *I Ching* or any of the other methods they may use to concentrate their thoughts. They will simply use whatever works and accept that the workings of the world will never be completely understood.

One more important point about Pagan magic should be stressed here, and that is that the standard rule applies, that nobody should be harmed. Pagans will not cast spells to hurt others, or to bend them to their will. A love spell can be cast to bring love into someone's life, but it will never force someone to love someone else if they do not want to. Pagans cannot put curses on people or cause harm to come to them, because doing so would break one of the only rules we have, to make sure that nobody is harmed as a result of our actions.

The First Rule of Paganism: There Are No Rules

Pagans have no hierarchy of authority. No Pagan is entitled to tell any other Pagan what they must do. We respect those who offer to share their wisdom with us, and revere them as teachers, but ultimately we teach each other, and ourselves. This book, and this very sentence within it, are merely suggestions and thoughts to ponder. The authors are merely friends in faith, writing down their thoughts for a wider audience. We are no more qualified to teach you than you are to teach us, but if you read our words and it encourages some thought or action on your part, then we thank you for doing us the honour of listening.

Although the anti-authoritarian aspect of Paganism means it shares a few principles with the anarchist movement, most Pagans are not anarchists. Many begin their interest in the religion as solitary seekers, using books and their own self-knowledge. Ultimately, though, many find themselves forming or joining a wider Pagan organization. Some fluctuate between group and solitary activities, others quickly find the way that suits them best and stick with it. There is no single *right* way to be a Pagan; there are as many Paganisms as there are Pagans.

Some Pagan organizations have developed a kind of education system. Many Wiccan covens, for example, confer 'degrees' on their members once they have reached a certain stage of knowledge and ability. The exact approaches vary, although the standard seems to involve three levels of achievement, possibly followed by recognition as an Elder. However, there is more to Paganism than pieces of paper; all they really mean is that one has 'done time' with a particular group. Nor are mere coincidences of heredity enough to confer power and authority. Simply because your parents are high priests it does not mean that you will inherit their mantles. You must work for it, just as all the other members of your group are striving to better themselves. Nature is about the survival of the fittest; Paganism is about exercising your spiritual and mental fitness until you are one with Nature itself.

Many have ridiculed Pagans for their beliefs and traditions. Pagans have long been thought of as somehow inferior spiritually, because their tradition is not as 'mature' as the patriarchal hierarchies of organized religions. Organized religions have also often thought Paganism to be a threat, and in a way it is – not to religion itself, because it is part of Pagan culture to revere, respect and listen to the beliefs of others, but to the organization. Pagans cannot be controlled like sheep in a pasture, cannot be forced to come to confession. Paganism is not a religion that rests on past glories or authorities. It is concerned with living a good life in the present day, and making the world a better place. Pagans are not concerned about where we have come from, only where we are going. Some like to claim a line of inheritance extending back into the distant past. Others care little for the patchy evidence of vaguely related traditions from the past, and prefer to accentuate modern Paganism's commitment to ecology and liberty. All religions, to some extent, grow out of the science and worldview of the times in which they are defined and codified. Christianity, for example, is 2,000 years behind the times, because it insists on the philosophical foundation of an old book. Paganism's strength is that it is a religion for today and all our tomorrows. It does not try to legitimize itself through nebulous connections with a doubtful past. Some Pagans use imagery from the past in their rituals, but this is for the impact these ceremonies have on our mundane selves. We understand that the Earth is not flat, that it is not the centre of the universe, and that the sun is a star.

This means that Pagans are not threatened by observers who wish to examine our history. As the next chapter will show, we have had our fair share of mistakes and misguided souls, but it does not matter. What matters is that we strive to make the world a better place, to be kind and loving to each other, and to free ourselves from mundane concerns through our golden rule: 'If it harm none, do as you will.'

3 Pagan Traditions

L ike all religions, modern Paganism is practised in a variety of ways, generally called traditions. Within these traditions there are separate sects which have split away from the main body, often as a result of personality clashes or differences of interpretation. Unlike other religions there is no set body of doctrines with the force of Holy Writ, handed down through the ages, and no revealed wisdom enshrined in a book. Compounding the confusion still further, there is a large number of Pagans who owe no allegiance to any particular group, but who have inevitably been influenced by one or more of the established traditions.

Paganism does not seek to convert and is generally tolerant of the beliefs of others, although as a result of persecution by Christian fundamentalists it has become much more assertive of late. However, until recently there has been a lot of mutual antagonism between the various Pagan traditions, which greatly hampered the formation of a unified religious movement. In the past, it was often difficult for an interested person to make contact with Pagan groups, but there are now a number of organizations prepared to provide information about their activities and also contacts for interested parties. Some of these groups are listed at the back of this book, along with some useful magazines, but the selection is by no means exhaustive.

To be a Pagan, however, there is no need to join any group, and the serious seeker can opt to follow an independent path. Indeed, many Pagans begin as self-initiates, or solitary seekers who learn the basics through books and self-instruction. They may contact an organization when they feel they have learned all they can alone, but some remain solitary practitioners, and others may even progress through several stages of isolation and group work, changing the style of their Paganism as they grow, learn and change. There are many folk within the wider Pagan movement who began as members of an organization, which

helped them to make a start, and who have then drifted away to simply
enjoy the freedom of self-determination.

This chapter gives details of the main traditions within Paganism, but
we obviously cannot discuss all the minor variations in ritual practice,
deities worshipped and conditions for admission. Moreover, since this
book is about the religion as such, lodges of ceremonial magic and
groups who practise variations of Aleister Crowley's occult teachings
have not been included. They would not necessarily describe themselves
as Pagan, although they may have Pagan members and in Wicca especially much of the ritual used has been adopted from ceremonial magic.

Wicca

As invented by Gerald Gardner, Wicca has been the prime force behind
the development of neo-Paganism in various countries, and has since
split into a number of different sects. Essentially, a Wiccan is a neo-Pagan
who practises ritual magic and regards him or herself as a witch engag-
ing in witchcraft. All witches are Pagans, but not all Pagans are witches,
and many Pagans outside the Wiccan movement will try to avoid the 'W'
word. For them it has too many associations in the mundane world with
evil and Satanism, and is hence more trouble than it is worth. However,
despite the negative connotations of warty noses and flying on broomsticks, many fine Pagan folk are proud to call themselves witches (men
and women alike – the word 'warlock' has negative connotations of its
own).

There is some evidence of hereditary and traditional witchcraft still in
existence, often handed down through families, but such folk tend to
keep to themselves, do not use any written material and are not necessarily witches in the 'modern' sense. They are better described as practitioners of Shamanism (see below), rather than witches in the Gardnerian
tradition.

A problem, albeit a minor one, which some Pagans have with the
Gardnerian tradition lies in the fact that although its heart was in the
right place and it has spawned a vibrant, good-hearted community in
the modern world, its founder often used doubtful sources and ideas. It
is easy for scholar or academic to demolish the spurious nature of
Gardner's sources, but the fact remains that what he produced appeared
in the right place at the right time. One can perform the same exercise
with any religion, but that does not invalidate it in the eyes of its adher-

ents. Gardnerian Wicca is still a vital force in Paganism, although many groups have adapted his original rituals, excising the fake medievalism and toning down the blatantly sexual, and sexist, emphasis. Many modern-day Pagans will happily admit to being drawn into the religion through the works or followers of Gerald Gardner, but will then go on to say that not everything he said was true.

Far from being a weakness in Paganism, many see such an admission as a shining example of its strength. What other religion could blithely write off some, but not all of its founder's teachings? What Christian sect would dare acknowledge that the teachings of Jesus were wise and good, but that St Paul's sexism and misogyny should be taken with a pinch of salt? And what a wonderful world it would be, if Christian, Jew and Muslim could happily mix and match the beliefs of their religions, accepting and glorifying differences instead of persecuting them. Paganism is all about self-discovery and self-belief. The divine shines through all of us, and not merely through the pronouncements of a chosen few. Many Pagans accept Gardner's contribution while acknowledging that he was also a product of his times. To err, of course, is only human. To be true, dyed-in-the-wool Gardnerians, however, as opposed to more eclectic witches, a group must follow the pattern of worship and rituals laid down in his *Book of Shadows*.

Gerald Gardner claimed to have been initiated into a coven of traditional New Forest witches just before the outbreak of the Second World War. He wrote that they had taught him the secrets of what he called the Craft, an expression obviously borrowed from Freemasonry but which is generally used by many Pagans to define their religion, even those where traditions are not necessarily Gardnerian. Research by Doreen Valiente, who was an initiate of Gardner's, has established that a women called Dorothy Clutterbuck was involved with the coven, but as both she and Gardner were members of an amateur dramatic troupe in Christchurch called the Rosicrucian Fellowship of Crotona, it is far more likely that they were middle-class occultists rather than hoary old witches. In 1949, Gardner published an indifferent novel under the title *High Magic's Aid*, in which he described the initiation of a witch. He followed this in 1954 with the famous *Witchcraft Today*, in which he claimed he had been permitted by the witches to reveal some of their secrets. This book was quite successful, and helped to put Wicca on the map, as well as establishing Gardner as a personality and pundit. However, his love of publicity eventually rebounded when interviews with the popular press were distorted into tales of black magic and Devil-worship.

Gardner founded his coven in the early 1950s, and it met at his London apartment or at a hut near a St. Albans naturist camp of which he was a member. He seems to have picked up the term 'coven' from reports of a seventeenth-century witchcraft trial in Scotland. The term comes from the Latin *conventus* (as in 'convention'), possibly through the Old French *couvent*, meaning 'gathering'.

Internal differences and disagreements eventually caused a split in the organization but to be a true Gardnerian, one must trace one's chain of initiation back through to one of the early members. The publication by Farrars of the original *Book of Shadows*, however, inspired a number of individuals to form their own covens, initiate themselves and adopt the title of 'Gardnerians'.

The best description of Wicca is undoubtedly *Wicca: The Old Religion in the New Age*, written by Vivianne Crowley, a very gifted high priestess who also happens to be a qualified psychologist. In general terms, it describes itself as a nature-based fertility religion which some refer to as the Old Religion, a term which is true only in the sense that it draws its inspiration from a variety of ancient sources. It is also a mystery religion, in that entry into Wicca is by way of ritual initiation into the Pagan mysteries, which also confers membership of the priesthood upon the initiate. Most covens feature an Outer Court in which those seeking admission can gain some training, take part in simple rituals, meet the other members and be assessed as to their suitability. In keeping with Gardner's love of archaisms, a potential member must wait for a year and a day before initiation into the Inner Court and knowledge of the secrets of the Craft, a subject which is dealt with in Chapter 13. In most covens, there is likely to be a development path consisting of several 'degrees', each representing a number of years of study and contribution to the group. Eventually, after a period of time that varies from coven to coven, the initiate can hope to become an Elder.

Common to Wicca is the practice of natural folk magic and an interest in such matters as divination and healing for beneficial purposes. It is recognized that every human being has levels of psychic ability that lie untapped in most people beneath the surface of their personality. Wiccans worship a Goddess, named Aradia by Gardner after the deity in Leland's book, and a consort horned god, usually named Cernunnos, who was in fact a Gaulish deity. The coven is run by a high priestess, who takes precedence over her co-leader, the high priest, who may or may not be her earthly partner. Wiccan rituals are carried out within the confines of a magic circle or sacred space and generally at night, in keeping with the Goddess-oriented worship of the moon. Meetings generally take place at the full moon with ceremonies known as Esbats, and the eight festivals outlined in Chapter 7 (which they call Sabbats).

The problem for the new seeker who becomes interested in Wicca is how to judge the quality of a coven which he or she may approach, as there are many which have simply set themselves up, taken on fancy titles and are interested in the religion for the wrong reasons. Such covens are usually dominated by a male with an over-large ego and an unhealthy interest in recruiting attractive young female members whose clothes he wishes to remove. That may sound unkind, but our own early experiences with a Wiccan coven were distinctly unfortunate and we have heard of similar problems from a number of female acquaintances. However, apart from the lunatic fringe, there are many covens which are extremely well organized and which offer both wise teaching and a warm family atmosphere, far removed from the 'bitchcraft and bicker' which has become part and parcel of many groups.

There are several other forms of Wicca which are ultimately derived from the Gardnerian inspiration, notably the Alexandrian. If Gerald Gardner was a product of his life and times (the Masonic emphasis on secrecy, the naturist emphasis on nudity, the friend-or-foe mentality characterized by his early years in the Home Guard and, indeed, the 1950s sexism), Alex Sanders was even more so. He claimed to have been initiated by his Welsh grandmother, who allegedly drew blood by nicking his scrotum with a knife, but he was in fact initiated by a woman witch from Sheffield. During a visit to Gerald Gardner on the Isle of Man, he was permitted to copy out the original *Book of Shadows* and subsequently formed his own coven with his wife Maxine as high priestess. Sanders was a showman and desperate self-publicist who soon became a 'rent-a-witch' for many journalists, whom he allowed to photograph supposedly secret rituals. Look at any popular book on the occult and you will find, under the heading of witchcraft, photos of naked folk dancing, most likely from the Sanders coven. Spurned as a mountebank by the Gardnerians, his tradition became known as Alexandrian, but it differed very little from Gardner's original except that it tended to be somewhat more ritualistic.

One great service that Gardner rendered was that through his emphasis on the worship of a Goddess and the role of a high priestess, he enabled women to develop their own spirituality and take their rightful place at the altar. However, while his ideas had the seed of egalitarianism in them, they were still flawed. Few modern Pagans, for example, even within the Gardnerian tradition, are prepared to dethrone their high priestess when she ceases to be 'young and beautiful', as he originally suggested. But to give him his due, in the early days of his coven, when all the Wicca in the world knew each other by name, he genuinely may not have given much thought to the future path of the Pagan tradition. There are many Gardnerian Wiccans of the 'baby boomer' generation who have been forced to introduce their own variations on reverence for older members of the coven. Indeed, some even have a degree of initiation above Elder called the Crone, for whom advanced old age is an extra mark of wisdom.

However, some female witches have sought a form of 'affirmative action' against Gardner's sexism. This has led to a feminist variation of Wicca known as Dianic, which started off in the United States. Some Dianic groups will admit men as members or associates, but others totally exclude them and are largely lesbian in character. It was only natural that after centuries of oppression by male-led religions, the feminist movement would find a spiritual haven in the new belief pattern known as Wicca and in love of the long-forgotten Goddess. However, in rejecting the male just as so many of our ancestors denied the female, such groups can lose the essence of male/female polarity which is so crucial in creating a harmonious balance between the genders.

Druidry

The original Druids were the priesthood of the Celts, acting as poets, lawmakers, judges and royal advisers. As their tradition was an oral one we have only a vague idea about their training and religious practices, largely based upon Latin accounts, but it is clear that their influence was paramount in ancient Celtic society.

Roman authors such as Tacitus, Pliny and Suetonius reported on the attempts of the Emperors to stamp out 'the religion of the Druids', which spoke of altars of human sacrifice, far removed from the pacifist religion of today. The later arrival of the Anglo Saxons pushed many ancient peoples to the edge of the former province of Britannia, where pockets of the Druidic tradition survived in the Celtic fringes of north-west Gaul or Brittany, Wales and Ireland. In Ireland, there is evidence that many members of the Druidic class simply embraced Christianity, becoming the backbone of the scholarly Celtic church, with a suspiciously pagan wheel of the seasons encircling the Celtic cross. With the triumph of medieval Christianity, memories of a barbaric Celtic past faded, and it was not until the late seventeenth and eighteenth centuries that the interest of scholars and antiquaries was awakened. This interest was triggered by curiosity about such ancient sites as Stonehenge and Avebury, with which the Druids became eternally linked in the popular imagination, although all the available evidence points to their worship being conducted in sacred oak groves and beside streams. The Druidic industry was born, and Druidry was invented as a form of wish-fulfilment by pious Anglican clergymen.

In 1792, on the day of the autumn equinox, a group claiming to be Welsh bards assembled on Primrose Hill in London to perform a ritual. With old Druidry's emphasis on songs and poetry instead of written records, such folk had continued as vagrant performers during the Middle Ages. Their practices had no religious significance, but they had maintained a platform for the Welsh language and culture. One member of this group was a Welshman who took the bardic name Iolo Morganwg, and it was he who was responsible for the outright forgery of a corpus of purported early texts. In his enthusiasm he instituted the annual pomposities of the Gorsedd ceremonies of the National Eisteddfod, complete with ornate ceremonial garb and sonorous verse. Since then, the Archdruid has frequently been a member of the Christian clergy, and such harmless activities have done much to enhance the knowledge of the Welsh language and culture.

In Pagan terms there are a number of Druid groups which tend to subdivide from time to time and reinvent themselves, but most are now represented by the Council of British Druid Orders. Some offer teaching and are more esoteric, while others have a back-to-nature stance, eschewing the robes and trappings of 'traditional' Druidry. In fact, anyone who follows the Celtic mystic tradition can call him or herself a Druid and attract disciples. In France, there is a strong interest in the subject, and two mutually antagonistic groups exist. Generally speaking, most Druids follow the eight-fold cycle of festivals described in Chapter 7, and tend to worship Celtic deities in a celebratory rather than a magical way. Unlike other Pagan traditions, Druidry has always been tolerated, often with wry amusement, by the general public, and its ceremonies treated on the same level as morris dancing on the village green. In keeping with the myth that associates Druids with Stonehenge, various groups have held dawn ceremonies there at the summer solstice, which in turn attracted hordes of hippies to the accompanying rock music festival. The latter was banned by the authorities in 1985, amid false claims of damage to the stones themselves, and as a result there have since been annual clashes between the police and would-be worshippers. Nevertheless, in spite of the spurious claims to antiquity, several serious Druid groups do exist and form a vital part of the Pagan community.

The Heathens

During the so-called Dark Ages after the end of the Roman occupation of Britain, successive waves of invaders came from the continent, bringing with them their own pantheons of gods and goddesses, which mingled with the traditions of the old local deities until they were all superseded by Christianity. The invaders and colonists were from various Germanic tribes, and pushed the Celtic British still further into the extremities of the island. Pagans today can naturally feel an affinity for the Celtic pantheon, especially if they have Celtic ancestors, but there are many British folk who feel more of an affinity for the Germanic deities, and groups have begun to cater for them as part of the general Pagan revival. Some refer to this Norse–Germanic tradition as 'heathen'; the word is often interchangeable with 'pagan', but has a northern European origin. One general term for the tradition is Asatru (derived from *Aesir-troth*, or belief in the gods), which is a legally recognized religion in Iceland. There are also individual traditions in Finland, and there has recently been an upsurge of interest in the newly liberated Baltic States. Other adherents of the broad tradition prefer to refer to themselves as Odinists, and they are strongly represented within the Pagan community in Britain and the United States.

The first real awakening of interest in Germanic Paganism occurred at the turn of the century in tandem with the *Wandervogel*, rambling clubs that revolted against city life. Their members went off into the countryside, sang folk songs, praised nature and sought out the roots of their own culture by living the simple life. Unfortunately the emerging Nazi movement was also in search of a spiritual foundation and eventually corrupted Paganism by harnessing it to serve the interests of the *volk* myth. The swastika, a Pagan symbol, became its emblem, and the SS adopted runic images for their badge. Although, or perhaps because, the system was unspeakably evil, its leaders were unbalanced, none more so than Himmler, who poured money into research projects about Atlantis and reconstructed castles as Pagan temples for the master race. Sadly,

Odinism still retains a whiff of its Nazi past, as well as being associated with re-enactment groups dressed up as Vikings, and it is only recently that many Odinic groups have seen themselves as, and been accepted as, a valid part of the Pagan movement. Odinists prefer to call themselves Heathens, but in revering one god above all others, risk being regarded as Monotheists. Their tradition is also regarded by some as too Nordic for the United Kingdom; Odin, after all, was also known as the Anglo-Saxon Woden, and some would prefer to revere him in this incarnation. Despite these wrangles, there are several Odinist groups in Britain, broadly similar in theology but differing on points of detail.

Odinists celebrate what are termed Blots, the rituals performed at various times of the year. Odinism is not an initiatory religion; instead its members make a profession of their faith, which involves the swearing of an oath. They are organized in hearths (like the Wiccan covens), and although there is in theory no bias against women, they tend to be more male-oriented than Wiccan covens, for example. As Odin, chief deity, received the runes after an ordeal hanging from a tree, working with the runes is a central part of Odinist activity, although it is also practised by other Pagans as a form of divination. The basis of the whole modern theology is the *Prose Edda*, a book written down in the thirteenth century by an Icelandic scholar. Odinists place great value on the Noble Virtues, which they list as courage, faith, honour, fidelity, discipline, industriousness, self-reliance and perseverance.

There are two groups in the UK who call themselves the Odinic Rite. They revere 'faith, folk and family' and, although it is not a central tenet of their faith, they have claimed that while all the world may be united in a spiritual desire for Paganism, different ethnic groups should keep to different ethnic gods. This, they stipulate, is not a racist belief, but a simple statement of common sense in order to avoid confusion and misinterpretation of the religions of other cultures. However, some extremists regard it as giving them *carte blanche* to refuse members from ethnic minorities and discourage racial miscegenation. While the majority of Odinic members do not subscribe to such politically incorrect views, their religion may face serious ideological stress in the near future. Just as Gardner's Wicca had to separate their founder's hits from his misses, the Odinic Rite must determine where they stand on 'half-caste' members and the all-too-obvious point that all religions, and indeed all races, are born of miscegenation and the contact of different cultures.

Already the Odinic groups cannot agree on Odintru (reverence of

Odin) against a more general Asatru (reverence of the Nordic pantheon) or indeed Vanatru (the reverence of a different set of Nordic gods), and the more recent Odinic Rite (which dates from 1989) stresses that its pronouncements and publications are guidelines as opposed to religious dogma. And although Odinism is undoubtedly Paganism, insofar as it is an old folk tradition and unChristian in nature, its genetically defined exclusivity is a little unsettling to Pagan believers who choose to emphasize ecology, one world, and by extrapolation, one world family. Moreover, many of the British and American Odinic people especially are bound to have some Anglo-Saxon, British or Celtic blood in them at the very least, and yet seem to have no trouble integrating with the full-blooded Odinic people of fully-Scandinavian descent. It would appear that some groups are more 'ethnic' than others.

A relatively small heathen tradition, the Odinshof, has managed to deal with many of these anomalies to form a far more 'Pagan' kind of Heathenism. Like the Odinic rites, it is organized in hearths, but it leaves room for both Odintru and Asatru. The Odinshof view is that Odin is a major teacher and leader within the wider pantheon of Norse gods, a position not dissimilar to the position of Buddha and the Buddhist tradition within Hinduism. The Odinshof also celebrates the eight-fold Pagan festivals of the year, and welcomes members from other ethnic and philosophical backgrounds. Although other Odinic traditions also place a value on the importance of the environment, the Odinshof does so more than most, to the extent of buying up tracts of woodland to restore them to a natural state. In all these regards, they are closer to Wiccans or eclectic Pagans than they are to the racially defined orthodoxies of the other Odinic traditions. Some members of the Odinic Rites have criticized the Odinshof for this. In fact, however, by shedding the exclusive trappings of its origins, the Odinshof has managed to reform Odinism into a viable religion. Like the witches who took Gardner at his spirit and not his word, the growing membership of the Odinshof has strengthened its tradition by being brave enough to examine it critically.

There are other Heathen organizations run along similar principles. Particularly powerful in the American tradition is the Rune Gild, an organization that has coalesced around the writings of two prominent Pagans. Emphasizing divination with the runes and a Shamanic tradition for invoking the Norse Gods, the Rune Gild is also very up-to-date. Their *Drighting* (high priestess), Freya Aswynn, compares the worship of deities to the Windows screen on a computer, claiming that they are merely artefacts for enabling us to relate closely to the unknowable divine. The Rune Gild is also more liberal in its approach to ethnic minorities. Although the entire point of ethnic pantheons is arguably to display some kind of generic racial emotions within a given group, the Rune Gild is happy to admit anyone who feels that there is something within the Norse tradition that speaks to them. For the Rune Gild, revering Odin above, say, Diana is not a racial issue, but simply a form of religious access that works best for them.

One strange offshoot of the Nordic tradition is Seax, or Saxon Wicca, which is a system simply invented by Raymond Buckland when he imported Gardner's Wicca into the United States. He set out his ideas in a book entitled *The Tree*, and it has been suggested that he did so as a joke. Nevertheless, his system offers a form of self-dedication and a series of simple rituals that can be performed by anyone alone or in a group, and they are just as valid as a ritual written by anyone else. Paganism is about personal freedom of choice, and Saxon Wicca is just as valid as any other tradition.

There are other groups within the Nordic tradition, but they are very small – we know of amateur dramatic societies with larger memberships than the British Rune Gild – and it is not feasible to devote a lot of space to minor differences in beliefs in a book about Paganism as a whole. It is, however, worth mentioning the Hammarens Ordens Sällskap (HOS), a Heathen movement that truly straddles the borders between spiritual Paganism and secular ecology. A self-sufficiency movement that worships the Earth above all things, and sees deities merely as vectors for contact with the paranormal, the HOS rejects many widely accepted traits of Heathenism as being later Christian inventions. They claim, for example, that the concept of Odin as an 'Almighty Father' was merely a Christian shorthand for what was observed in northern Europe, and not a true reflection of Odin's role in the Norse tradition. Some of their ideas are truly fascinating: their perspective on Paganism shares many characteristics with Zen Buddhism, in that many of their 'sacred cows' are only sacred in the eyes of their detractors. They point out, for example, that many Heathens helped in the destruction of the Uppsala temple around AD 1100 not because they had become Christian converts, but because they considered the temple as no more than a building. If the Christians would leave them alone for the next several hundred years, and the only price was the demolition of a single temple, they willingly agreed. So the event was not the missionary victory that the misguided Christians believed. As part of the HOS tradition, there is considerable emphasis on environmental care, and although the movement is currently very small, its all-embracing attitude, its combination of the secular and the religious, and the potential it offers for multi-denominational worship (by admitting that all gods are symbols) makes it a movement with true unifying potential for Pagans in the twenty-first century.

Shamanism

This is a tradition that is almost impossible to define – more difficult even than Paganism itself. This is because the discussion of Paganism normally involves at least two people talking over ideas; Shamanism, on the other hand, needs only one person and a universe to be in. *Shaman* is the Siberian word for a tribal sorcerer (female *shamanka*) and such people are found in almost every society, from the Inuit to the Australian Aboriginals, from African peoples to Hindu fakirs and Central American Indians. In the West, the word has become a catch-all expression for those who have the ability to move 'between worlds', be it through ecstatic drumming, chanting, meditation or any other stimuli. In many cultures, the state of ecstatic trance was induced by hallucinogens in the form of mushrooms or another naturally occurring plant. This tradition is as old as mankind; certain individuals developed the ability to enter the spirit realms and thus become a form of tribal 'priesthood' as witch-doctors, prophets and seers. One of the earliest religious icons in human history is a picture of a dancing man dressed in the skin of a deer, found in the Trois Frères cave in France, his purpose being an act of sympathetic magic.

Shamanism in the West today is not exactly a religious neo-tradition like Wicca or Odinism; it is really more of a solo pursuit, but it is widely practised, especially in the United States, where it is even taught in workshops. During the 1960s there was a strong interest in the religion and culture of the North American Indians among young Americans, coupled with an even greater interest in psychedelic drugs. People discovered that LSD produced similar effects to the peyote mushrooms popular in Central America with Shamanic practitioners and serious academics wrote books about drug-induced trance states. The actual practice of Shamanism thus has strong overtones of the American Indian beliefs and uses much of their language, such as totem animals and spirit journeys. Ceremonies such as smoking pipes, often filled with substances other than tobacco, communal sweat lodges and 'smudging' with herbal smoke have been absorbed into Shamanic ritual.

The practice of Shamanism came to Britain from America and surfaced among New Age folk, hippies and others who found the ceremonial aspects of Wicca not to their taste. They were the sort of people who were travellers in the original Peace Convoy, and others who went out to commune with Nature with drums, often seeking out ancient sites to contact ancestral spirits. Original writers such as John and Caitlin Matthews have produced a more home-grown version of Celtic Shamanism and there is a thriving industry turning out traditional Irish drums. The aim of drumming is to induce a trance in which the Shaman 'travels' on a visionary quest. During this quest he or she is shown symbols and can enter into conversation with mythical beings or be guided by animals. It is an experience that anyone can participate in through experiment, and it is very much part of the rituals of the road protest movement, for example. Forms of Shamanic practice have been transported into other disciplines or were already part of them, such as the Wiccan way of raising power by dancing and chanting in a circle. Initiates of Wicca who worship Celtic deities could thus describe themselves as Druids, but could also incorporate a number of Shamanic practices. Paganism is full of such cross-fertilization, which has enriched all the traditions.

Other Groups or Organizations

By its very nature, Paganism defies any attempt at imposing rules or dogma, but as we are all social animals to a degree, there is a tendency at times to band together for a common purpose. There are numerous organizations which represent special interests within the community, such as animal rights or gay Pagans, and others which transcend boundaries or deal with networking. It would take a whole book to describe them all in detail, and in describing the following we do not necessarily imply that they are better than others; they simply give a flavour of the community.

One of the most popular of the wider groups is the Fellowship of Isis, which is based in Ireland and claims a membership of over 11,000. It was dedicated to the reintroduction of the worship of the Goddess in all her aspects and in all cultures, and is thus theoretically attractive to Roman Catholics who revere Mary the Virgin. Attached to the Fellowship is the Druid Clan of Dana, which offers a valuable introduction to Druidic beliefs and practice. The Fellowship offers tuition through groups known as lyceums, which form the component parts of the College of Isis and ordination into the Pagan priesthood for suitable men and women.

One of the authors, Anthony Kemp, is involved with a smaller group, the Order of Brighid, which is public in the sense that anyone can join if they believe in the basic principles of co-equal male and female deities, respect for nature in all forms and acceptance of the law to do as you will, if it harm none. A few of the hearths can offer tuition by experienced members, but it is basically an organization founded on friendship, to keep folk in touch with others and to encourage a more open attitude towards Paganism. Another organization which puts people in touch with each other is Paganlink, a networking body which has been going for a number of years and has a regional organization. The Pagan Federation is a truly international body, which publishes an excellent magazine. It is the 'respectable' voice of Paganism, able to represent the community to the media.

A fairly recent development has been the strong interest in eco-magic, in which the power of magic is harnessed towards healing our planet. The Pagan Federation sponsors an annual Earth Healing Day which is widely supported, and a vital organization known as Dragon devotes itself to practical healing work. It is common for the media to regard the current road protest movement as being a bunch of long-haired and unwashed dropouts from society, eager to provoke violent clashes with the police. True, there is an anarchic element, but there are also vast numbers of decent and concerned Pagan folk who are involved, and the same applies to the recent spate of demonstrations against live animal exports to the continent. Even earlier, Pagans were to be found in the ranks of the Campaign for Nuclear Disarmament and in the Green political movement.

Anyone who scans the small advertisements in the various Pagan magazines will find workshops and courses on a variety of topics, and the Order of Bards, Ovates and Druids even offers correspondence courses in its own tradition. John and Caitlin Matthews, referred to above, offer courses in Celtic mysticism, and Vivianne and Chris Crowley do likewise for Wicca. Only a few years ago, information on Paganism was extremely difficult to come by. Today, however, Pagans are more vocal and open, and no longer so resistant to publicity and attention. Long may that remain so as we move into the Aquarian Age of personal choice and freedom of religious expression.

4 First Steps

Having found out about some of the many traditions that make up the Pagan community, the next question is: What do Pagans actually do? There is a short answer to the question and a long one, and as with all questions about Paganism, the ultimate decision about which you choose rests with you. It is enough for you to *feel* that you are a Pagan by sentiment, and to lead a fulfilling life by concerning yourself with the well-being of others and caring for the environment to the best of your ability. After all, there are many worthwhile Christians who have never seen the inside of a church. This chapter, however, is designed for those who feel they would like to explore the spiritual and religious side of Paganism for themselves, but do not necessarily wish to become involved with any particular group or tradition, at least for the time being. There are many hedgewitches around who work alone or with a couple of friends, and all of them had to start somewhere.

Getting started can be quite daunting, as many seekers will have to put aside a whole set of preconceived notions that have been drummed in over the years by parents, teachers and the representatives of less open religious traditions. Many may feel that they require a teacher, and will wonder how they should set about finding one. If you decide to become involved with a group, it will offer teaching, the quality of which will depend upon the ability of whoever is in charge. It will also, of course, reflect the particular tradition of that group. The truly fortunate will not have to concern themselves with these questions; a priestess or priest will take them in hand at the right moment and give them the support they need.

Once safely on the path of self-awareness, the Pagan novice can then hope to learn from the wisdom of a whole variety of people. The only qualification required to become a Pagan teacher is whether or not the students are prepared to listen. There is no such thing as 'instant knowledge', and Paganism encourages students to approach their beliefs critically. The Eastern concept of the guru is quite foreign to Paganism, which stresses the individuality of each seeker's quest; and one cannot gain enlightenment by sitting at the feet of a guru for twenty years. We have yet to meet a hippy from the 1960s who made the trek to India to study in the ashram of one of the fashionable gurus of the period who came back with any great enlightenment. Most spent their time getting stoned.

We also urge students to 'shop around' a bit, and to beware of any group that claims to have access to exclusivity of the 'truth', whatever that is; some covens do not even permit their members to socialize with other Pagans, which is perhaps an indictment of their leaders' insecurity. If a teacher is right for you, he or she will appear. But this book is about *practical* Paganism, and to make the right teacher 'appear', you must make sure you are looking in the right place. No matter how powerful your spells, the chance of the right teacher knocking on your door by chance is remote indeed. Make yourself known.

What Do Pagans Read?

Judaism, Islam and Christianity are so-called 'revealed' religions, based on the word of their God as revealed to a prophet or written down in a holy book. Luckily, Paganism does not have such fetters and a vast amount of literature is available, presenting often diverging viewpoints as well as a rich store of knowledge. Sadly, the notion of Paganism, especially witchcraft with its popular imagery of spell-casting and power, will always attract hacks intent on capitalizing on people's insecurities. Many occult outpourings are quite turgid and others are full of outright untruths and sheer stupidity, but the critical Pagan novice must learn to make his or her own judgements on good and bad. Nobody can make that judgement for you, because you are your own boss in the Pagan tradition.

You should read everything you can lay your hands on, apply your critical faculties and never believe anything you read in print unless you have tried it out for yourself and found it to be worthwhile. In preparing the bibliography at the end of this book, we have resisted the temptation to make a blanket list of everything we have ever read on the subject, and have concentrated on a selection of titles that we regard as honest, straightforward and informative for those who are new to the path. Most Pagans of our acquaintance are voracious readers and compulsive book collectors, and no knowledge is ever truly wasted. It is better to have read up on the subject than risk being influenced by the Pagan pub bore.

What Do Pagans Charge?

Most Pagans would regard it as immoral to charge for anything they provided in the nature of spiritual teaching or magical help such as a healing ritual. If a decent Pagan priest is asked to bless a child or celebrate a marriage, he would not usually demand a fee, but would regard it as reasonable for his travelling expenses to be paid. There are organizations which charge fees for teaching material, but before parting with your money it is best to find out first what is actually being offered. Anybody with more money than sense can 'buy' a magic degree or a high rank in some fake-occult organization. And anyone reading the pages of various New Age magazines may well be bewildered by the vast array of so-called 'workshops' that are on offer, as well as the amazing array of alternative therapies that can heal everyone's problems – for a fee.

Attending a few workshops can be a worthwhile experience, and there are some extremely capable teachers of such disciplines as sacred dance, meditation, holistic massage etc., as well as a number of well-run residential centres. Local authority evening classes are also a useful source of enlightenment on subjects such as astrology, mythology and the Arthurian legends. We have, however, from time to time come across a certain type of individual who attends a different course each weekend, a bit like a train spotter darting from station to station. They have seen it all and done it all, yet somehow have not found satisfaction or their own key to enlightenment. The same applies to the compulsive therapy addict, who will consume any kind of alternative lifestyle, without ever *really* listening. At Glastonbury one could spend a month being treated morning, noon and night, never repeating the same therapy, and still depart with one's 'problems' intact. We are not knocking alternative medicine as a whole, but the whole area has been swamped by psycho-babble and pseudo-psychic therapies offered by practitioners who have little or no qualification. And by qualification, of course, we mean a genuine ability. Pagans, remember, are not impressed by mere pieces of paper.

Do Pagans Pray?

Yes, of course they do; invoking our gods and simply talking to them is a basic part of human nature, and always has been. The difference between us and the established religions is that there is no prayer book as such, although many beautiful prayers, invocations and poems have been published in a variety of books and magazines. The best thing is to start your own prayer book by copying out anything you read which strikes you as particularly suitable, or which triggers an emotional response. In order to keep you focused on worship, multidenominational Pagan prayers that leave a blank space for the deity should be copied out with your chosen deity's name inserted. When you are praying, you want to concentrate all your attention upon the prayer, not upon remembering where you saw the prayer first, who wrote it, or for whom it may have originally been intended.

Having gained an insight into the prayers of others, try writing your own. You do not have to have a degree in literature, as anything is heard if it is said sincerely. You may find that by drifting into a meditational state, the necessary words simply come as if dictated by your subconscious.

Pagans can pray anywhere at any time, both for others and for themselves, but their methods vary greatly. Some prefer to kneel and clasp hands in the Christian manner, a perfectly acceptable ritual to focus the mind and show respect for the divine. Others sit cross-legged and meditate like the Japanese, emptying their minds of all thoughts and waiting for the divine to come to them. Still others will simply commune with nature, enjoying the beauty of the world around them, and becoming one with it through sheer happiness. The only important common factor is sincerity; otherwise, try whatever works for you. A beautiful song is more spiritual than a gabbled string of 'Hail Marys', as is a piece of handmade pottery crafted with love in the heart.

Where Do Pagans Worship?

The Pagan community in the United Kingdom does not have any 'churches' as such, but many of the American groups have formed themselves into worshipping bodies based around actual centres. There is an essential anarchy about Paganism which tends to resist anything in the way of artificial structures and strictures, hierarchies and dogma. Most of those who call themselves Pagans prefer to work alone or in small groups, the membership of which is fairly elastic. There are a number of organizations listed in the Appendix, but these are generally for the purpose of disseminating information or putting people in touch with others of similar interests. Paganism is not a centralized religion, it is a local affair, so local that the names of our gods change from town to town.

In the early days of Gardnerian Wicca, for example, no provision was made for increasing group size, because the members of Gardner's first coven never gave it any thought. Many American covens now set down rules early in their life that the coven must be split if numbers ever rise above a certain limit. It's not that Pagans do not want their religion to be popular, it is just that the Pagan definition of 'popular' is not a giant ritual in a stadium where the people at the back cannot see or hear what is going on at the front. Small, flourishing groups of like-minded, friendly people seem to be the Pagan norm; large impersonal gatherings are not in keeping with the spirit of our tradition.

A fairly recent and very welcome feature of the wider Pagan community has been the rapid growth of what are generally called pub moots, which are listed in many Pagan magazines. They generally meet regularly on a given date (such as the first Friday of the month), and give like-minded folk in a particular area a chance to get to know each other. Some, like the popular Talking Stick meetings in London, feature a speaker, while others are simply an opportunity to have a good chat and a beer with friends. In a similar vein, open rituals have been held in some areas, as well as informal picnics. The virtue is that anyone can go along, but if they do not like the people involved, they can leave. Any movement will attract its fringe of ego-trippers, charlatans and complete lunatics, and the Pagan community is no exception. Each of us, however, is endowed with a healthy critical faculty which is there to be used. If you are seeking nothing more than a prop or a crutch then Paganism is not for you; indeed, you would be better off with a belief pattern like Christianity, which specializes in offering certainties on a plate.

Pagan worship can be as simple or complicated as you wish; it all depends on your temperament or means. Some people are quite content to go to wild places alone, dressed in their ordinary clothes, to weave their magic silently and commune with nature. Not everyone, however, has access to Nature on a regular basis, or can live the good life in a log cabin by a tranquil lake. Those who live in towns and cities have to create their temple inside a building, which can be anything from the corner of a bedsit to a specially dedicated and magnificently appointed room. As Paganism is all about Nature and our relationship with the natural world, most Pagans believe that ritual activity is best celebrated outdoors where possible, but in northern Europe, poor weather and a short summer tend to mitigate against this. We remember one occasion when we were invited to join a Shamanic group on a trip into the woods in November. An hour later, in spite of layer upon layer of clothes, we were soaking wet and thoroughly frozen. No amount of drum-banging and chanting could induce a sense of spiritual purpose; instead, all we could think of was a nice warm room with a log fire and soft candlelight.

Where we live in France Nature is all around us and we have a secluded orchard, but land in Britain is expensive. Some groups have obtained permission to use other people's land, and one coven in Milton Keynes actually persuaded the council to allow it to work rituals on municipally owned land. Ancient sacred sites exercise a strong pull, but those wishing to worship at Stonehenge, for example, have fallen foul of government regulations, and the monument tends to be avoided by Pagans these days; we simply object to paying to look at the stones through a fence. Various Druid groups still work openly at sites in London, such as Tower Hill, and at Glastonbury, without causing public outrage, and this is perhaps the best policy to adopt. After all, there are many less spectacular venues, such as ancient burial mounds or barrows, springs, wells and hill forts. All these attract Pagans with their sense of past worship, and as you travel about you can often detect traces of their passage – a piece of ribbon tied in the branches of a tree, the stub of a candle or a wilted flower as an offering to the old gods of the place, perhaps even the remains of a fire.

We all carry our own temples around in our minds, and there is no need for a suitcase of equipment. At one Wiccan gathering in a Sussex woodland, we witnessed the high priest unpacking a huge array of wands, swords and other paraphernalia, but that simply is not necessary. However, for those of us who have to work indoors, a pleasant space conducive to spiritual activity helps greatly as an aid to concentration. In an ideal world it would be nice to have a house large enough for a room to be devoted specifically to worship, but this is seldom the case. But with a little ingenuity, any room can be converted into a temple, including the lounge or a bedroom. All that is needed is sufficient floor space for the numbers present and a small table to use as an altar. Simply push back the furniture or move it outside into the hall and you are in business. In our experience, rooms which are regularly used for Pagan worship acquire a very special ambience of their own, which makes spending time in them a warming experience, whether it is in a council flat or a suburban house.

What Do Pagans Wear – If Anything?

The subject of ritual nudity is one of the hoariest old chestnuts of popular folklore, and we have all read headlines in the tabloid press along the lines of 'naked witches in midnight forest romp'. To be a Pagan, however, you do not need to remove your clothes, so do not worry on that score. Some groups believe that nudity plays an important role in certain rituals, but today, with our modern taboos, the sensible Pagan has to weigh the pros of ritual togetherness against the cons of distractions, embarrassment and lechery. For many Pagan groups, ritual nudity is simply more trouble than it is worth, and this is a perfectly acceptable position.

Gerald Gardner was a passionate naturist, and foisted his own predilections on his Wiccan movement. He justified this by quoting a passage in Charles Leland's *Aradia: The Gospel of the Witches*, in which Maddalena, a Tuscan witch, is supposed to have told the author: 'Naked shall ye be in your rites.' However, that is no reason for imposing his fantasies of dusky Mediterranean maidens upon the real world of a serious religion. There is considerable doubt about the general authenticity of Leland's book, and besides, nude magic on a warm Italian evening is a lot easier to deal with than nude magic at midnight in Newcastle in the November rain.

Nudity as such is a problem for many folk who have been brought up within the Judeo-Christian taboo structure, which emphasizes the vileness of the human body, but this was not so in the ancient world. In Greek and Egyptian iconography, a fertility god was portrayed rampantly erect, and the Greeks themselves worshipped the naked body without the need for modest figleaves.

Deciding to worship naked, either alone or in company, has certain advantages. Clothes have long been used to hide bodily deficiencies, convey wealth or imply status, and when such clothing is removed it becomes harder to pretend or dissemble. Nudity is democratic, in that nobody can exhibit the latest fashion, except perhaps for their taste in jewellery. Arguably, it is also an important component of the ritual preparation, reminding the participants that they are about to embark on a ceremony of power and gravity, quite separate from the mundane world of suits and shoes. However, that in itself is no argument for compulsory nudity. The donning of ceremonial robes is just as much an equalizer of social status and a symbol of great moment, and this is the method favoured by some Pagan groups, especially in the United States.

It is frequently claimed that the naked body enables energy to pass more easily, but we fail to see that the forces of Nature, which can destroy towns, set fires in forests and wash away cliffs, would be much deterred by a thin cotton robe! Personally, we have worked with several groups who worship naked, or 'skyclad' as Gardner called it, and can vouch for a heightened sense of mutual awareness once all physical barriers had been removed. Without clothes in the circle, the colour of the skin, the chubbiness of the tummy and the presence of stretch marks all cease to be important. All that, however, presupposes a close group of friends who love and trust each other enough to be naked together, and there is no place for the lone voyeur.

If you find yourself in a Pagan group that does not worship skyclad, those who work in the open often prefer to wear normal clothes for self-protection, perhaps with a cloak over the top, except when the summer is warm enough for a light dress or robe. Druids have a formal attire and headdress, the colour of which indicates the wearer's rank within the order. The design has nothing to do with ancient Druidic costumes, and owes far more to nineteenth-century romanticism, with trouser-legs poking out underneath. Lodges which practise ceremonial magic tend to go in for quite fancy sets of robes for different occasions, and these can prove very expensive. That said, most Pagans own some sort of robe which they use for ritual purposes.

Whatever is worn should be made from a natural fibre such as cotton or silk, and that applies also to anything worn underneath. Acres of nylon underwear are hardly conducive to feeling natural, and the robe is only a covering for the naked body. You can buy ready-made robes from specialist suppliers, and what you wear is a matter of taste and budget. It is best to start off with a simple, plain white robe which can be run up from cotton sheeting and is openable down to the waist, with or without a hood. Other colours can also be worn if you prefer, and any robe can be decorated with embroidery, lace or other adornments. An inexpensive alternative is a long T-shirt, which is very suitable for children or women – like the old-fashioned cotton Victorian nightgown – or you can simply wrap a piece of material about yourself South Pacific style. Other useful sources of ritual clothing are Indian shops, which sell relatively inexpensive silk dresses as well as long, plain loose shirts for men. Also useful is a length of cord to bind around the waist, which can be purchased from department stores that deal in haberdashery or upholstery accessories. In effect, whatever you wear – or do not – is strictly personal, except when you join a group that has adopted a dress code. It should also be stressed that ritual garments should only be used for their particular purpose and otherwise be kept in a safe place.

In addition to ritual clothing, there is the matter of jewellery. Many Pagan women have special necklaces, bracelets, ankle chains and rings which they wear when worshipping. These tend to be silver as that metal is sacred to the moon. Such items should also be kept separate from everyday jewellery and not be handled by others. Different gem stones have traditional sacred or astrological attributes which may well affect your choice. Men can also wear jewellery if they want, and a necklace made of acorns is one suggestion. There are many craftspeople who make beautiful Celtic pattern jewellery, and who advertise in the Pagan press. Ours is a joyous religion and most people like to dress up. Our Pagan ancestors had a great love of display, and our gods want us to be happy when we worship them, rather than remain sober and miserable. Esoteric tattoos and nose studs are quite common among those folk who seek a tribal identity separate from their modern social background.

Nowhere is it more true that you cannot judge a book by its cover than in Paganism. Take a random sample of Pagans at worship and you will see an incredible cross-section of the population. At the subliminal level, they may be country ladies out walking their dogs, enjoying the beauty of nature. In their tweeds and wellingtons, they are Pagans at heart, although they may never realize it. They may be well-dressed professionals donning over-robes before a ceremony to remind themselves that they are about to take part in an extraordinary ceremony that will separate them, however temporarily, from the humdrum nature of their everyday existence. They may be housewives who meet for weekly coffee mornings before worshipping their favourite goddess in ceremonies that may have become more boisterous since several of them had children. The solitary hedgewitch in her caravan, eking out a subsistence living on the outskirts of the town, is another kind of Pagan, seeing eternity in her vegetable patch, and aiding the local people with her knowledge of natural herbs. The scary youths at a protestors' camp are Pagans, adorning their bodies with piercings and tattoos, and writhing to the modern rhythms that are somehow also as old as tribal dances. All these disparate groups and more are part of the rich tapestry of Paganism. It is impossible to identify a particular kind of clothing that they share, or a particular characteristic by which they can be recognized, but this is all to the good. Do not look for jewellery or a badge, do not look for a neon sign over someone's head announcing that you can talk to them about witchcraft. You must search for subtler signs. Look at what they are reading, watch their attitudes toward others, listen for the way they speak to you. The superficialities of a dress code or a particular form of identification are beneath Paganism. Look with better eyes than that.

5   Consecration and Dedication

The ancient Romans had shrines to their household gods and modern Pagans have something similar. At its very basic level, such a shrine is a space where you put things that are special to you, such as a feather found on a walk, a stone from a beach, some crystals and seasonal offerings of nuts, seeds and flowers. It can be a small shelf, the mantelpiece or a table in the corner. To it can be added a vase, candlesticks, an incense burner and figurines of a totem animal, a goddess or a god. Items such as a container for salt, a water jug and a small pot of consecrated oil may prove useful for some of the rituals described later in the book. There are shops that supply such things but you do not have to go out and buy a young Pagan's magical mystery kit in a box. When we started out, we found that the right items seemed to present themselves when the need arose, probably because our minds had decided to look for them. Almost everything we treasure was either bought in a second-hand shop or given by friends. If you have a dedicated temple space, the house shrine will probably do duty as your altar, but if not, the altar will have to be laid out each time it is used. Ensure that other people do not touch your special things without your express permission, as negative vibrations are easily transferred. Unless you are sure of the people you invite into your space, it is best to keep the shrine out of the way, as it is not a suitable surface for ashtrays and coffee mugs.

Ritual 'Tools'

In addition to purely decorative items, which most Pagans seem to acquire in some quantity, there are a few essentials for ritual purposes. In Wicca, Gardner laid down a whole list of what he called the working 'tools' of a witch, a term borrowed from Freemasonry. These included a black-handled knife or *athame*, a white-handled knife, a cup, a wand, various cords and a scourge. Traditionally, it was regarded as essential that such items should be handmade by their owner, but these days not all of us have the necessary handicraft skills.

For basic ritual work you will need a cup or chalice in which the libation is consecrated. It is symbolically feminine, representing the womb and the cauldron of rebirth, and it should never be used for any purpose other than sharing the ritual wine (or other drink). A knife or sword is symbolically male, representing the generative power of the penis, and is never unsheathed in anger. Legendary tales are full of references to magical swords and cups, which are simply allegorical of male–female polarity. The Grail was borne by a virgin priestess and the knights who sought it had powerful magical swords. To emphasize his right to kingship, Arthur had to pull the sword from the stone – a definite symbol of virility. In practical terms, a ritual knife as a personal weapon is a matter of individual preference, and becomes an extension of its owner's hand (remembering to 'harm none') as well as symbolizing initiation within a coven. Pagans who feel the need to brandish weapons are reminded of the Sikh tradition, which calls for all the faithful to carry a sword at all times, but is conveniently vague about how large the sword must be. Some Sikh 'swords' are little more than key-rings.

Some Pagans prefer a wand in addition to or as a substitute for a knife. Hazel is a popular wood, and the traditional length is from the owner's elbow to the tip of the fingers. It can remain plain, be carved with symbols or even wrapped with ribbons. To cut a wand, choose a tree and ask its permission to take a piece from it. Using a sharp knife, cut a single shoot of roughly the right length as cleanly as possible. When you have done so, thank the tree for the gift and leave an offering in return – a lock of your hair perhaps, or a coin buried among the roots. Any trimmings from the shoot should be burned rather than simply thrown away. The same rules apply to taking wood for a staff, which is another popular Pagan accoutrement, especially among those who spend a lot of time outdoors.

Incense is pleasing to both gods and humans. But finding the right type can be a problem, and many folk are quite content to make do with joss-sticks, which are freely available in a variety of fragrances. Alternatively many Asian shops sell small cones of incense that can be burned in a saucer on a bed of sand. This is a suitable vessel for any burnable incense, as the sand takes away a lot of the heat and reduces the fire hazard considerably. The best incenses, which unfortunately are not readily available, are those which come in a powder or crystalline form, and are sprinkled on specially produced charcoal blocks, which can be placed on a saucer of sand or in a special burner like a censer used in a church. Again, such burners, made of brass and fitted with chains, can often be found quite cheaply in Indian shops, but they do tend to get very hot indeed, hence the chains. There is a wonderful emporium in Glastonbury called Star Child which markets a whole range of hand-mixed incenses and has a mail-order service. They have fragrances dedicated to various gods and goddesses, for each of the major festivals and for the different planets and astrological signs, as well as for special purposes such as meditation and healing.

Preparing for a Ritual

Having decided to set up a house shrine or altar it is time to celebrate your first ritual, which can be quite a nerve-wracking business as it is you who must do it – not the vicar, the minister, the imam or the rabbi. But this is part of Paganism's central message: you are in charge. There is no such thing as an exhaustive list or a 'right' way to do things; a personal shrine is, after all, a personal matter.

It is essential to choose a time when you know you will not be disturbed, and to unplug such secular distractions as the telephone. Pagans tend to work in the evenings, but this is merely a matter of taste or convenience and the daytime is equally valid. However, most Pagans agree that a darkened room lit by candles is more conducive to the right frame of mind than daylight and outside noises.

Any items you intend to use for rituals should be cleansed and consecrated, and emphatically not used for any other purpose. Ritual cleansing removes any negative energies that may cling to an object, whether purchased new or second-hand – you simply do not know where it has been! The easiest method of cleansing is to hold the object under running water, or, even better, in a spring or fast-flowing stream, at the same time imagining it to be washed and purified.

Once you have washed any items to be consecrated, dry and then polish them (it is amazing how much metal polish a practising Pagan can get through). It is now time to cleanse and purify yourself before consecrating your altar or shrine and the items on it. It is a good idea first to ensure that you have everything ready beforehand. Make sure your surface is safe and clean and perhaps cover it with a cloth, whether it is a small table, a shelf or the mantelpiece. The cloth can be white or any colour you prefer, plain or with finely embroidered symbols such as a pentagram, a Celtic cross or the Egyptian Eye of Horus. Place all the items to be consecrated on a separate table and check that you have everything: candles, incense, some salt, water, flowers, etc. Also make sure you have the matches handy, as it is far more satisfying to kindle a naked flame than merely to spark up a lighter.

When everything is in place, it is time to cleanse yourself. Many folk these days only have access to a shower, and while there is a wonderful sense of invigoration underneath the running water, a shower cabinet is a difficult place to meditate, especially if you are juggling the hot and cold taps. A bath is better in that you can spend some time stretched out in the warm water and let your thoughts roam free. It is even more spiritual when the bathroom has a joss-stick burning and is lit by candlelight. Pagan bathrooms tend to be sweet-smelling and welcoming places decorated with sea shells and other water-inspired objects.

As for the bath itself, it is best to make sure it is as unique and special as the occasion that is to follow it. Put some essential oils in it or hang a muslin bag of herbs under the hot tap. All of this will help to induce a feeling of well-being. When everything is ready, undress slowly and with deliberation, feeling that as you remove each garment you are also shedding the mundane cares of earning a living, bringing up children, making a happy relationship or whatever. You may like to try the following combination of herbs for your ritual bath:

Place the following dried herbs in a muslin bag in the approximate proportions shown:

Rosemary: 7 Parts
Lavender: 7 Parts
Basil: 5 Parts
Lemon balm: 2 Parts
Plus small amounts of valerian, sage and fennel

As a further refinement, before getting into the water take some pure rock or sea-salt crystals and cast them into the bath, saying as you do so:

Thus shall this water be cleansed so that I may be made pure. May the spirits of water be present to guide my thoughts and bless me.

When you have finished and dried yourself, to make the point that this is a very special occasion and that you are a very special person, you should take some perfumed oil and anoint yourself with a dab on the forehead, chest, palms, genitals and soles of the feet for there is no part of us that is not of the gods. The final step is to don your robe, ensuring that anything you wear ritually is clean. As you do so, feel the sense of occasion that accompanies the donning of your magical personality. Take the folded robe and hold it in front of you, saying:

> May this robe be blessed, the outer symbol of my inner purity of spirit. As I wear it, may I be clothed in light.

Put it on deliberately and slowly, feeling that you are reclothing yourself in preparation for encountering the divine and naturally wishing to look your best. Then take your cord, and before encircling your waist with it, hold it up in offering with the following words:

> May this, my cord, the symbol of all earthly ties that have bound me, remind me always that I am free.

All these ritual actions may sound complicated, and even portentous and unnecessary, but each is a valuable aid to concentration. They exist to enhance your sense of purpose as you consecrate yourself to worship with dignity and respect for whatever deities will be invoked. You may well be performing your ritual in a corner of a living room full of reminders of everyday things, but the ability to see your sacred space in your imagination as a beautiful temple will greatly enhance the power of anything you may wish to do.

Consecration

Before you perform the ritual, you should consecrate everything that will be used, including the robe and cord you will wear. A suitable time for this is after your first ritual bath, when you can perform the rite naked or clad in a clean dressing gown. Collect everything that you are going to use somewhere convenient, and have ready some pure rock or sea salt, a bowl of water (preferably spring water, ideally collected direct from the spring), a candle and some burning incense. First, ritually cleanse yourself so that you can consecrate the artefacts.

SAMPLE RITUAL FOR CONSECRATION OF YOURSELF

May this water cleanse me, that I may know the divine.
May this salt purify me that I may know the divine.
May the incense bring freshness, that I may know the divine.
May this flame sear away impurities, that I may know the
   divine.
Thus am I free to do my will, if it harm none.

Then take each item and sprinkle it first with water, then with a few
grains of salt. Pass it through the smoke of the incense and over the
flame of the candle. As you say the words below you should imagine
the desired effect being implanted into the inanimate object. What is it
for? To provide light in your temple. So visualize it as warm and glowing in your mind. Visualize a water bowl as filled with a deep, clear
pool, into which you gaze to find intuitive visions. See the salt as soaking up impurities and negativities, and the incense as suffusing the air
around it with joy. These are merely suggestions; you can easily make
up your own.

SAMPLE RITUAL FOR THE CONSECRATION OF THE CANDLE

May this water cleanse you, that you may light my temple.
May this salt purify you that you may light my temple.
May the incense bring freshness, that you may light my
   temple.
May this flame sear away impurities, that you may light my
   temple.
Thus thou art consecrated to my use.

SAMPLE RITUALS FOR THE CONSECRATION OF OTHER ITEMS

May this water cleanse you, that evil may be washed away
   (etc.) (*for water*)

May this water cleanse you that you may purify my temple
   (etc.) (*for salt*)

May this water cleanse you that your fragrance may fill the air
   (etc.) (*for incense*)

Creating a Sacred Space

Some method of creating a sacred space is used in all Pagan traditions, some of which use highly complicated rituals which they have lifted from the dubious old spellbooks of the ceremonial magicians. These come complete with arcane symbols and Hebrew letters which are supposed to drive off demons. The gentle and natural rituals outlined in this book are hardly likely to attract hordes of malicious hobgoblins intent on devouring the unwary, but nevertheless, creating a magical working space promotes a sense of ease and of being 'between the worlds'. If you trawl through the available literature, you will find several methods of 'casting the circle', which is the Wiccan term for this universal Pagan practice. It is, however, something of a misnomer, because what is actually being created is not a circle but a *sphere*, inside which the participants are suspended. The consecration ritual which follows is simple and sincere, requires a minimum of paraphernalia, is easy to perform and will work anywhere, both in or out of doors. It can also, of course, be embellished to suit your individual preferences, as you gain more experience and gather new sources of inspiration.

When you and any other people present have duly bathed and robed yourselves, enter the place where the ritual activity is to take place. As a bare minimum, you will need four candles in individual holders, which should be placed at the cardinal points of the compass, each of which is also symbolized by one of the four classic elements: east for air, south for fire, west for water and north for earth. It is even better to have a set of candles coloured according to the elemental colours: blue for east, red for south, green for west and brown or orange for north. In addition to the candles at the quarters, you can also place symbols: a feather in the east for air, an incense burner in the south for fire, a bowl of water in the west and a lump of rock salt for north. On the altar table you will need your consecrated rock or sea salt, bowl of water, incense burner and candle. When working out of doors you can omit any of the above, as candles blow out and you may not have the other items handy in a carrier bag while wandering through the woods – or even sufficient privacy. The Wiccan tradition calls for the altar to be in the north, but in the more general magical tradition it should be in the east, where the sun rises and the gentle winds blow in inspiration. If, however, you are working to gain intuition, why not place your altar in the west, to encourage the influence of the element of water? Similarly, if you wish to encourage vigour and passion, you can place it in the south, to summon forth the element of fire.

Once you are in the proper place, everyone present must centre themselves. Sit in a circle and slow your breathing by setting a rhythm of counting silently, three in and three out. As you do so, close your eyes and feel the blood circulating in your body. Do your best to cut out any disturbing noises and imagine yourself in a beautiful setting – a magnificent temple of a woodland glade dappled with warm sunshine, for example. If you are outside, you will be able to tune in directly to the natural sounds all around and feel the solidity of the earth beneath you. Once you feel that you have relaxed, try pulling in the earth energy, which is easier if you are sitting on the grass rather than a carpet. Sense the concentration of power that lies in the genital area, and consciously pull up the energy from beneath you. This will cause a glowing energy at the base of your spine. Then imagine that energy travelling up through your body via your stomach, solar plexus, heart, throat, forehead and crown, flooding you with warmth and bright light so that you are sitting in a glowing silver aura. Try it – it works!

Now you are ready to consecrate your space. Starting in the east, light the quarter candles in a clockwise order, and finally the altar candle, saying as you do:

In the east, let there be light.
In the south, let there be light.
In the west, let there be light.
In the north, let there be light.
In this our temple, let there be light, love and understanding.

At the same time, light your chosen incense and then sit for a while soaking up the atmosphere of the candlelight and the sensuous smell. If there is more than one person present, all should take turns at consecrating the space, or share out the various tasks and phrases so that everyone can gain some experience of the ritual working. The first step is to request the presence of the guardians of the four elements, again a tradition which comes from ritual magic, but is in general use among Pagans, remembering that they are powerful forces and they are not to be *summoned* from their distant realms. Rather, they elect to attend your meeting, honouring you by their presence, and you should treat them with respect. Each person will have their own image of the Lords and Ladies of the Elements, but the following is a suggestion.

For the element of air, see the colour blue and imagine yourself standing on a bare mountain top with a strong but sweetly scented breeze blowing across your body. In the distance, a mountain range of vast rock-hewn beings looks down upon you. For fire, visualize the colour red and look into a vast, glowing, burning pit of fire, sensing its cauterizing, purifying energy. Water is the colour green; visualize a pool of deep, dark green water, into which you gaze, or perhaps a vast tinkling waterfall in a distant landscape. Earth is best seen as an orange/brown, and you might like to picture a vast ochre desert stretching away to distant mountains. Again, start at the east and work clockwise, stand with your legs apart, imagine the scene you wish to visualize and invoke it. Turn to each of the directions, breathe, visualize and invoke each spirit:

> Lords and Ladies, guardian powers of air,
> I entreat you to send your cleansing winds,
> To protect my/our blessed circle this night.

> Lords and Ladies, guardian powers of fire,
> I entreat you to send your blessed warmth,
> To purify my/our blessed circle this night.

> Lords and Ladies, guardian powers of water,
> Allow me/us to gaze into your crystal pools,
> To enlighten my/our blessed circle this night.

> Lords and Ladies, guardian powers of earth,
> I entreat you to lend your steadfast ground,
> To ward and protect this space tonight.

What you have just done is build a strong link with the elements who will be standing guard at each quarter. Pause for a moment and visualize them all around you, for the next stage is to invoke the presence of your chosen deity or deities.

The one golden rule here is not to mix pantheons. If they are working a healing, some people may invoke Thoth the Egyptian or Hermes the Greek, perhaps the Celtic Cerridwen, but not all three! You might argue that it should not matter, that the gods of all cultures are aspects of the same ultimate divinity, that everything eventually is just a mask for the all-encompassing male and female principles of the universe.

Indeed, that much is true, but in dividing these principles into lesser deities, more manageable 'chunks' of magical power, we cannot mix our metaphors. To use one trite example, let us imagine that we are trying to calm the storms overhead. Whom do we invoke? That will depend on which tradition we are rooted in, but we have many choices. Let us also suppose that we are part of a group that contains members who know the pantheons of just two traditions, northern Europe and ancient Greece. The Norse Thor is the god of thunder (amongst other things), while in the Greek tradition, thunder is the prerogative of Zeus, the father of the gods. However, in the Norse tradition the father of the gods is not Thor but Odin. So by mixing traditions, we would also be mixing our messages. The gods have different strengths, and represent certain forces within their own traditions. The whole reason that we are invoking them is to concentrate our minds, and our attunement to Nature and the job in hand. By mixing traditions, we are not focusing at all, but confusing the issue still further. Gods and goddesses are the ultimate embodiment of certain forces in the universe. It has taken each culture centuries of development to create the archetypal beings that form its pantheon, a slow sculpting of many lifetimes that whittles the life experience of an entire people into a group of superbeings. How arrogant we are to think that we can mix and match as if we were picking out sweets in Woolworth's. It is better to concentrate your efforts on a single tradition, rather than confuse your and your fellow worshippers' minds.

If you can hold more than one tradition in your head at once, then by all means worship different pantheons on different occasions, but the chances are that if any pantheon does not fill all your needs, it is probably not the right one for you. This is why many Pagans prefer to go 'right to the top' in the chain of gods and goddesses, and deal not with the culturally defined deities of our ancestors but with the generative principle of the universe itself. It is vaguer, but it is also more unified and accessible to disparate worshippers.

You may choose simply to invoke the Great Mother and her consort, perhaps seeing them as Pan and Diana, or Cerridwen and Lugh. Stand or kneel before the altar and prepare yourself. At that moment, and for that moment, you have become a priest or priestess, ritually bathed, purified and clothed in your robe, your whole being flooded with light and love. You are about to create a space that is between the worlds of gods and humans. Feel your own nakedness beneath the thin covering and recognize your own insignificance, but realize that you too are truly beautiful, a child of the Lord and Lady.

You do not need lofty phrases and bombastic fake medieval language to invoke your chosen deities. Talk to them with respect and humbly ask them to be present in your space, and to support your work. Your work should be clearly described as the aims of your prayers, perhaps healing for a member of the group, or a bountiful harvest from your fruit garden. If you are sincere, yet unsure about the words to use, ask for help and you may find that the right words will come of their own accord. On the night of your self-dedication, you might simply say:

> Great Lady, Goddess of the Moon, and great Lord, Guardian of the Wild Places, I, [name], stand before you as a child, ready to be made pure and dedicated to your service. I do humbly entreat you to be present in this my temple, and to guide me, that I may find the true path that is right for me.

Having made your invocation, try to imagine the deities as hidden presences filling your temple with their power. If this is the first time you are creating a sacred space, you will probably be nervous, so pause for a moment and listen to the silence around you. If there are others present, brief them beforehand and get them to back you up with their own imagination in such a way as to create a bond within the temple.

When you feel ready, take your knife, wand or, if you prefer, simply your index finger, and stand facing the east. Imagine a brilliant shaft of silvery-blue light entering the crown of your head and flowing down through your outstretched arm. Move slowly clockwise, seeing the light you are projecting following you as you move, creating a flickering trace as you draw a circle through the south, the west and the north until you arrive back where you started. When you can visualize the circle you have drawn, move into the centre, seeing it all around you, and stretch out your arms. Then pull the circle up around you so that it forms a dome over your head, and push it down underneath your feet so that you are standing in a brilliant bubble of light. Hold that visualization for a moment and sense yourself and any others present as being isolated between the worlds in a timeless zone of beauty. You will in fact discover that time can slow down in the temple, and when you finish your working and re-enter the real world, you may find that what seemed to take an hour in reality took three.

If you have a small hand-bell, you can ring it three times to signify that you have completed your sacred space. Let the vibrations of the final ring die away into nothingness as a signal to those beings behind you. You are now ready to proceed with any ritual you intend to work. Some books on witchcraft place a strict prohibition on leaving the circle, and it is a good idea not to break it unnecessarily, but as I have said, there is no legion of angry demons prowling about outside. If you do need to leave it for any reason, or to admit someone, then you can cut an imaginary door in your mind and close it behind you afterwards.

Closing Your Space

Having created a sacred space, you must also close it down properly, otherwise any entities you have invoked can linger in limbo while you have packed up and blithely gone to bed. This is the spiritual equivalent of leaving all the lights on, and is extremely bad manners. Your space was created in ritual and respect, and should be closed with similar ceremony.

Repeat your opening actions in reverse order and in the reverse direction, anticlockwise. Standing in the centre, pull the imaginary dome apart, and as you do so, visualize the light gradually diminishing, to be replaced by the normal, ambient light of the room. Thank the deities you invoked for their presence and bid them return to their realms, saying:

Hail and Farewell.

Do likewise with the Lords and Ladies of the Elements, starting in the east and rotating anticlockwise, blowing out their candles as you go. Finally, blow out the altar candle, and, if you have a bell, ring it three times saying:

The rite is ended.

It is very important after a working to ground yourself. Sit for a moment in silence feeling your way back into your normal surroundings, and then have a snack or a hot drink or finish off the last of the wine. What you are doing is closing down your aura, which in the temple will have been open to astral influences which you may not wish to disturb your sleep.

A Ritual of Self-dedication

This was originally written to be worked in isolation, but it can be combined with the sacred space creation ritual. If you are going to perform it, the best idea is to write it out in the correct order and then file it for future reference. When two or more people perform their dedication at the same time, they can speak in turn or intone together. In this ritual, there is no complex magic-making involved, and the only entities invoked are those which lie dormant within each and every one of us if we have the courage to acknowledge them. It is not a form of initiation, nor is it a commitment to any particular denomination of Paganism. What it is is a personal dedication, and as such it should be entered into lightly. Any invocation of the powers beyond our material realm evokes an answer, not as a great clap of thunder, but rather as a quickening of one's own senses. Inevitably there will be a change in the seeker's life, imperceptibly at first but gaining pace with each new piece of knowledge that is added to the jigsaw puzzle of existence.

The main prerequisite for undertaking this ritual dedication is an absolute certainty that it is what you really want to do. If you cannot summon up that commitment then there is no point to the ritual, and it will not work anyway. The actual working is designed for a solitary worshipper, but it can also be carried out by a pair of friends or a small group who intend to study together. When you work will depend on a number of factors, but ideally it should be the night of a new moon, or perhaps one of the eight great festivals. Another possibility would be a birthday or a particular day associated with a goddess or legendary figure with whom you feel a strong affinity. Ideally, too, you should choose a day when you are free from work and can thus relax.

All you will need is a space of clear floor, a small table to act as altar and the absolute certainty that you will not be disturbed. The altar should be placed in the east, covered with a white cloth and decorated with a vase of seasonal flowers or foliage, a small bowl of water, some salt, a white candle, a goblet of wine and an incense burner or joss-stick holder. You will also need some anointing oil. Choose a natural carrier like pure olive oil or make one from almond kernels and add a few drops of perfume. A good one to use would be sandalwood. Place a few drops of the oil in a small bowl or dish.

You will need a robe, which can quite easily be made as a loose caftan-like garment with wide sleeves, and should be a natural fibre such as cotton. You can choose any colour you wish, although ideally for a new beginning it should be white. You should also obtain a length of plain white cord about 3 metres long. Finally, if you wish, you could have an amulet available to wear about your neck. This is your gift to yourself, and will be a constant reminder of your dedication to the path of pilgrimage.

To prepare yourself, spend as much of the day avoiding stressful activities. Take some time to go for a walk in as natural a setting as possible, tune in to the earth, and mull over what you are going to do. If you can, avoid eating until after the working, and keep away from alcohol in order to keep your mind sharp.

In the evening, make sure your temple space is warm and prepare your altar with love and care. Place your robe, cord and amulet on the altar if there is enough room, but do not light the candle yet. Make sure there are enough candles ready around the room to provide sufficient light and that the telephone is disconnected. Having checked that everything is ready, matches included, take a bath or shower and imagine that the water is washing you free of all the things you do not particularly like about yourself.

After the bath, enter your temple space completely naked. Wear no jewellery, perfume or make-up, and leave your hair hanging loose. Light the candles around the room and then the altar candle and your incense. Kneel or sit cross-legged in front of your altar and centre yourself by slowing down your rate of breathing and allowing each part of your body to relax. Sense the atmosphere, smell the incense smoke and gaze upon the flowers in the warm candlelight. Take as much time as you feel you need to attune with your inner self, and then prepare for the step you are about to take.

When you feel that you are ready, speak aloud or say to yourself:

Naked I came into this world and naked must I leave it. Thus I come before the altar as I truly am, prepared as a pilgrim to walk the path of self-knowledge. May my guardian spirit be with me to light my way.

Then stand up, take a pinch of salt and sprinkle it in the water, saying:

With this salt I do cleanse thee, that thou may purify me.

Take the bowl and lift it up as an offering. Then dip your fingers into it and sprinkle yourself. Take the incense, lift it in offering and pass it slowly over the front of your body, smelling the smoke before replacing it on the altar. Pick up the candle and repeat the movement, sensing the warmth of the candle on your skin. Feel that you have been cleansed by the four elements: earth, water, air and fire. Kneel before the altar and say:

Thus purified, I, [name], offer myself in humility and love as a servant to thee, Great Mother, Goddess of this Earth and all creatures that dwell upon it. Descend, I do entreat thee, and be with me in my waking hours and in my sleep. Open up my mind to receive that which I must know and let thy love and light enter into me this night. In thy sacred presence I do solemnly dedicate myself as a pilgrim to devote my life to thy service and thus to work for the good of this planet, my fellow beings and all thy creatures.

Remain kneeling for a while with your eyes closed and visualize the Goddess in your mind. Feel her presence and love entering your body, filling you with light and warmth. Then stand up and dip your right forefinger into the anointing oil. On your forehead make an equal-armed cross with oil and describe a circle around it. This is the ancient Celtic symbol of the elements in perfect balance, enclosed within the circle of death and rebirth. Say:

I anoint myself that my mind may be opened to receive that which I must know.

Anoint the palms of your hands:

I anoint my hands that all I touch may be blessed.

Anoint the soles of your feet.

I anoint my feet that my steps along the path shall not falter.

Anoint your genitals:

I anoint my womanhood/manhood without which we would not be. There is no part of me that is not of the Gods.

Duly anointed, take the robe and sprinkle it with a few droplets of the water and salt, pass the incense over it and then pass it above the flame of the candle, if it has not yet been consecrated as described above. Hold it up in a gesture of offering and then put it on, slowly and solemnly. Say:

> In token of this my dedication, I clothe my nakedness with the garment of purity. Robed as a pilgrim, I shall worship at the altar of the Great Mother and go forth from here with purposeful stride to fulfil my destiny.

Consecrate the cord in the same way, and bind it about your waist, saying:

> May this cord be a symbol of the earthly bonds I have loosened.

Take the amulet (if you have chosen one) and consecrate it. Then kiss it and place it around your neck, saying:

> May this personal symbol, never to be removed, serve to remind me always of my dedication this night, and may it serve to protect me from all that would deflect me from my chosen way.

Kneel again in front of the altar and take the cup of wine. Hold it up and offer it to the Goddess, as it is her symbol. Then drink it slowly, leaving a small drop at the bottom to be returned to the earth. Sit comfortably and meditate on the ritual you have just completed. Feel the material of the robe against your skin and the presence of the Goddess all around you. As you ponder, you may consider some particular course of action as a symbol of the commitment you have made, like joining a campaigning group or enrolling for a course of study.

When you feel that you are ready, kneel once again and, in your own words, thank the Goddess for her presence and for all that you have experienced. Blow out the altar candle, wrap it in a piece of clean cloth and keep it in a safe place so that you can use it again if you wish to renew your commitment at any time, perhaps every year. If you have a garden, take the remaining wine and pour it on to the soil, thanking the Goddess for her bounty. If you live in a flat you can make the offering to a pot plant, or put the wine into a small clean bottle and take it the following day to the local park, for example.

After the working, make sure you have something to eat and drink, to close down the aura and earth yourself. You are now a practising Pagan who has made a solemn commitment and are at the start of what will prove to be a fulfilling new stage of personal development. Blessed are all those who take that step.

6   Paganism as a Way of Life

You are now a Pagan; being a Pagan really is that simple. Everything still looks the same, of course. You still live in the same place, have the same job and hobbies. The world has not changed, but you have, and that is what being a Pagan is all about. It is all about self-improvement and self-awareness. It does not guarantee an end to suffering, easy riches or a perfect life, simply because you have signed on the dotted line. Paganism does not sell indulgences or allow pre-booking for front seats at Judgement Day. Its message to you is twofold: first, that in many ways you are on your own – your life is yours to live, yours to ruin and yours to win; and secondly, that now you have a huge group of friends and like-minded souls who are in the same boat as you. Some of them are Pagans, and they will understand. Some are non-Pagans, and living amongst them may cause difficulties.

Is There Anything I Am Not Allowed to Do?

The simple answer is no. Unlike other religions, Paganism does not define itself according to the restrictions it imposes upon its adherents. Do you feel like going to church? Go right ahead, learn from the wisdom of Christianity, and smugly note the damage done to it by two millennia of *human* failing. Note also, among the zealots and the witch-burners who occupy the lunatic fringes of any religion, the vast numbers of truly good-hearted, kind people. These Christians are not your enemies, they are fellow worshippers of the Cosmic All.

Pagans welcome the chance to examine other philosophies and incorporate their good points. Some Pagans actually belong to the hierarchies of other religious orders, and are Christian pastors one day and Wiccan high priests the next. Paganism does not see any dichotomy here, because they are both approaches to the same concept of the divine. It is Christianity that has mounted complex theological arguments against the incorporation of other faiths; Paganism welcomes everyone and everything.

Paganism is its own reward. There are no 'holy days of obligation' like those in the hard-line Church. We have our eight-fold cycle of yearly festivals, and it is to your own benefit if you attend. If you do not, you might miss out on the chance to greet old friends or meet new ones. But your spiritual connection to the divine will not be severed by your non-attendance. Do what you will, if it harm none.

Should I Tell Anyone I Am a Pagan?

Many Pagans choose a new name on initiation, and use it either within the closed circle of their fellow Pagans, or throughout every aspect of their lives. It is not fair to call them pseudonyms, since many Pagans would argue that their Craft name is their real, chosen name and the one they were born with was merely a temporary measure until they awoke to their true existence. Why the dual identity? There are plenty of reasons, even in this supposedly enlightened day and age, for Pagans to stay 'in the closet'. Not least among these are the associations in popular mythology between Paganism, witchcraft and Satanism. Anyone who takes the time to do their homework will know that Paganism is merely a religion that is not Christian (adapted, in the case of modern Pagans, to fit the definitions described in Chapter 2), that Wicca is a denomination of Paganism, and that Satanism is a completely separate, unrelated, perversion of Christianity. However, there is no guarantee that you will have time to say this, or to pass over a copy of this book. Some people will hear the word Pagan and immediately suspect you of moonlit sacrifices, church burnings and a secret responsibility for every unsolved crime in the neighbourhood. Frankly, can you be bothered to waste your time and theirs attempting to fight such ignorance?

You might find such ignorance to be a challenge, as many Pagans do, but remember that Paganism is not a proselytizing religion. We do not seek converts, converts seek us, and any attempt to explain the truth to an uninterested person is very close to missionary work. We do not do that; Paganism is about your own private development. There is no Pagan doctrine that finds you a better place in Heaven if you bring in new converts, so why bother even trying?

Matters become even worse if you describe yourself as a witch. The word has so many negative connotations today that it is often more trouble than it is worth. Say you are a witch in the wrong neighbourhood and you will be blamed for every tiny thing that goes wrong. Even worse, some of the more weak-minded individuals will come to you and ask you to work magic for them. In other words, they will want the spiritual benefits of witchcraft without the spiritual awareness it requires. If you try explaining to them that magic only works as part of a larger system of reverence and ritual, the argument is likely to go something like this. If a female friend asks you to make the man next door fall in love with her, you will explain that you cannot do it because if he does not want to it would constitute 'harm' and hence be prohibited under the Witches' Rede. She may then want to know what kind of magic only works if the subject wants it to, and you will have to explain that it will work if you do it hard enough, but that there will be a price. You can cast a spell to encourage her to meet someone special, but artificially forcing a couple together when only one of the parties genuinely wants the relationship will only lead to problems. You could 'get' the man next door, but things would inevitably go wrong and you would be blamed, not your friend's bad choice of love object. Such people are best sent away with a book to read, so that they can understand why you have refused them. In this case, it is not missionary work, it is an effort to stop harm from coming to you.

A more problematic area of requests for magic occurs when the person who makes the request is perfectly genuine. Instead of asking for some selfish desire like a love spell, he or she might ask for your help over a sick person of their acquaintance. You could turn such a person away, which would be unkind and probably bad public relations to boot. Or you could explain that you will 'say prayers' for the sick person at your next meeting. That ought to convey the right sense of meaning to your non-Pagan supplicant; it sounds as well-meaning and 'normal' as prayers in a Christian church, and essentially you will be performing the same sort of operation, and will be better received than 'Of course, we will work a ritual at the next full moon' or 'Yes, we will invoke our patron deity of healing, the goddess Cerridwen.'

Nobody truly understands the power of the human mind over mundane matter. Many religions acknowledge that simply thinking hard about something will help bring it about, probably by exercising your mind to think through the physical obstacles in its way. The Zen monks think that contemplating nothing will eventually result in an awareness of Something. The Buddhists believe that chanting over and over for something you want will help you focus your mind to go out and get it, though they add the caveat that you can chant all you want, but if you want to cook some rice you will have to put it on the stove. When it comes to more nebulous areas of affecting the world around you, an Indian rain-dance or prayers for the sick, it is a matter of faith. You believe that Something is out there, you believe that it can hear you (as a deity) or bring you some kind of power (as a force like electricity), but no religion has come up with a perfect interface for accessing the spiritual world. This is what makes a religion a religion instead of a science. We will cover 'workings' or ritual spell-casting later in the book, but for now it is best to bear in mind that your own link with the forces of Nature will be difficult to explain to someone else, especially if they think your magic is some kind of parlour trick. Keep your explanations simple, use terminology that they can understand, like 'prayer', and avoid words they will misinterpret, like 'spell'.

Within your own social circle there is not likely to be too much of a problem. After all, your friends will love you, know you and understand you. It is a different matter, however, in the workplace. The same issues that might turn your neighbours against you could be doubly troublesome in the office or factory. Unlike your friends, the mere fact that you regularly find yourself in close proximity to these people does not mean they will necessarily like you. In many working environments there are other pressures, such as jockeying for promotion or tenure, that may lead others to use any knowledge they have about you for their own ends. It can still be problematic in the workplace if you belong to an ethnic minority, have different sexual leanings, or indeed are nothing more threatening than a member of the opposite sex. Just think how much worse those undercurrents can be if your religious background is (however wrongly) associated with Satanism, sacrifices, spell-casting and curse-making.

Even if your workmates are genuinely supportive, the associations of Paganism may eventually prove to be a problem. Some people may even find your religious affiliation intriguing or impressive, so impressive in fact that they stop thinking of you as a co-worker and start thinking of you as nothing more than a Pagan. You will cease to be the fastest typist, most reliable manager or most trustworthy clerk. Instead, you will be 'the witch' or 'the Pagan', perhaps initially in awe or in jest. But this in itself is a type of discrimination and can bring dangers. If your workmates cease to rate you by your ability at your job, it may affect your promotion prospects. Equal opportunity should protect you from discrimination – after all you cannot be fired simply for being black, or gay, or female – but you may find Paganism treated differently. If you tell one person in your office, you should expect the news to get around, possibly to those who do not know you so well or do not know quite as much about your religion as your Pagan-friendly colleagues. Just because you think you have convinced the person at the next desk that Paganism is all right, it does not follow that the boss who is looking for an excuse to lay off staff will take the same view. Nor will the many hours you may have spent explaining Paganism to a sympathetic audience of friends be much help if you have five minutes to make your case before an industrial tribunal.

There are many Pagans who feel that this view creates a self-perpetuating pattern of discrimination. They argue, quite sensibly, that until Pagans are prepared to make a stand and 'come out of the broom closet', it is inevitable that ignorance and Christian propaganda will win out against the truth; fearful individuals will continue to suspect that we conduct terrifying rituals in private. To be honest, however, they would think that whatever we did to try to convince them otherwise. The texts of many Pagan rituals are freely available in bookshops, and our philosophy and worldview is the subject of many books, articles and television programmes, and yet we still hear all the old jokes about witches on broomsticks. Even if all our ceremonies were televised, the nay-sayers would still claim that we were keeping the evil material for secret, closed rituals.

However, things are slowly changing, and many Pagans are prepared to go public. Some will happily tell all to anyone who asks. Others make carefully prepared statements, or write and give interviews to suitable journals, either openly or under Craft names to protect their everyday existence and families. You may want to pursue this route or you may not, but ultimately your religious beliefs provide the answer for you: it is in the Wiccan Rede. You can do whatever you want, as long as it 'harms none', and in this case, we have to remember that the concept of harm also applies to ourselves. What personally, would be worse for you: bottling up a secret that you would rather tell your friends and family, or risking ignorant comment and persecution from others if you explain your religious stance before they are ready to hear it? Like any aspect of Paganism, it is completely up to you, but the best advice in the early stages is to do nothing rather than make a decision you may come to regret. You have no duty to Paganism to tell the world how much fun it is or to bring in new worshippers. Pagans' ultimate duties are to love themselves and those who love them. And if you have to share an office with a Christian evangelist, do as you would be done by and keep religious discussion off the daily agenda.

There is a tangential problem attached to the issue of 'coming out' as a Pagan, which needs to be mentioned simply so that you are prepared for it. A secretive religion, a hidden way of worship or simply a 'hole' in the conversation where a discussion of religious matters might otherwise have taken place can all take on an exaggerated importance and influence our view of the world and ourselves. Try not to think of the world in terms of 'us' and 'them', because it will encourage an antagonistic view that is quite at odds with Pagan tradition. You are not a member of the 'Chosen People' just because you have decided to become a Pagan. The god or goddess has not chosen you. Far from it, in fact, since by selecting a particular pantheon or approach to the divine, it is you who have chosen your god or goddess. Like everybody else, you are nothing more nor less than a member of the human race; you are not better or worse than a non-Pagan. You will meet good Christians, you will meet bad Pagans. No matter what labels you try to put on them, people will still be people. If you find yourself developing feelings of superiority, deal with them quickly. A Pagan world allows everyone to live together in harmony; there are no outcasts, and that means that you cannot cast out others, nor should you allow yourself to be cast out of their world (be it at work, school or the social club) because of something you do in the privacy of your own home.

Vegetarianism

One of the commonest questions asked of Pagans is whether or not they are vegetarians. Many are, and many take the philosophy further, becoming vegans or 'fruitarians'. They take the Rede very seriously, and point out that 'harming none' should really extend to animals and plants as well. However, some Pagans suggest that science has given us a better knowledge of the world around us, and that it is possible to take the notion of 'harm' too far; it is silly to expect a human being to go through life without harming anything. On the other hand, saying that some creatures may be harmed and others cannot creates its own problems and plants the seeds of discrimination. This philosophical issue is one of the thorniest questions in modern Paganism, because it is a reminder of our disparate traditions. We have eco-warriors who refuse to eat meat and witches who refuse to harm other creatures, but also localized god and goddess traditions rooted in Norse and Celtic hunting culture.

Every time we put our foot down, we destroy millions of microbes. Every time we breathe in, we inhale entire societies of germs. We cannot seriously expect not to 'harm' micro-organisms, because we do so with each breath and step we take. We could conceivably imitate the Jains of India, who go out of their way to avoid harming tiny creatures by wearing masks and filters, but this surely causes 'harm' to the individuals concerned by ruining their lives. There is a Buddhist principle called ahimsa, which states that the important matter in karma is whether or not you have deliberately contributed to the death of the creature involved. If you accidentally ran over a hedgehog on a dark country road, it would not be your fault, and so would not bring you any bad karma. If, however, you saw the hedgehog up ahead, accelerated, ran it down and then reversed back over it to make sure you had completed the job, you would have its death on your conscience. However, when it comes to eating meat, ahimsa does not save you from guilt. If you buy meat, you are paying the industry that provided it; in a way, you are handing a few coins to a man with a knife who is doing your dirty work for you. This makes you just as guilty as if you had slain the creature yourself.

Some neo-Pagans have thrown a few more facts into the argument. They point out, for example, that it is part of our natural evolution to be meat-eaters. Our teeth are equipped for dealing with meat and vegetables, we are omnivores. Meat-eating creatures in the natural world do not suffer for their natural inclinations; we do not blame the owl for eating mice or the wolf for hunting sheep. Our propensity for eating meat is part of our natural development, and living in harmony with Nature is part of the Pagan creed. Some Pagans, indeed, would prefer to return to the old ways of hunting in areas of forest and plain, since that would be far kinder to the environment than the depredations of agribusiness that have turned huge tracts of the countryside into chemical-sodden wastelands of artificially augmented wheat.

But it is important to keep things in perspective. Many of us could not be the people we are if we were not able to rely on others to gather our food. It is true that our ancestors were hunters, farmers and fishers, who lived in harmony with Nature. But they also lived with disease, disaster, famine, fire and flood. Nobody could spare any time away from the struggle for food, so they had no books, no medicines and no science. Some modern self-sufficiency Pagans would like us to return to a point in the continuum of human development, when tasks were less specialized. But they are still looking at one *point* in the continuum.

If you do not hunt or farm your own food, if you do not make your own pots, if you do not build your own house, you are agreeing to allow others to involve themselves in your life. Did your own job exist in ancient times, and if so, *how* ancient? To what point in the continuum should we return? If your job is a new creation, what part does it serve in the great scheme of things? Hardline Pagans might regard insurance salesmen as unnatural parasites, but who among our ancestors would not willingly have paid a fee to ensure that they would be kept safe and well? In many ways, this is exactly how many religions came to be born. The difference between modern, secular insurance and medieval religious indulgences is that there are at least some guarantees in the modern age. So insurance salesmen also have a place in the Pagan order; they have made the world a better place.

You may be wondering what this has to do with vegetarianism. The answer is that it is a question of our place in the modern world. Most of us are urban, sheltered, cosseted individuals. Compared to our ancestors, we all live in relative comfort and safety. We have turned many tasks over to others, and the modern economy and transport has taken a lot of the personal contact out of trade – we are no longer likely to know the person who butchers our meat or makes our pottery. But we do wield incredible power as consumers.

The practical Pagan attitude towards food is best summed up thus. The best kind of food is that which has been grown naturally, and which you have farmed yourself. If it is meat, it is best that you have killed it yourself. If you are buying your food from a supermarket, then organic vegetables and free-range meat are at least closer in their point of origin to the natural world than they would be if grown in tanks or beneath sprays of chemicals. If you decide to eat meat, why not consider the lessons we have learned from other religious traditions. Kosher meat is prepared with the animal's welfare as central concern. It is also available in any high street, so why not utilize the humane efforts of the rabbi? Also, although our ancestors were omnivores, they were prevented by practicalities from eating meat on any but the most special of occasions. Why not try and phase it out of at least part of your diet. If you like meat you will appreciate it and the animal's sacrifice even more on those occasions that you do eat it. Alternatively, you may discover that meat was not that important to you after all, and that once you stop eating it, you can happily live without it.

Ecodefence and Animal Rights

A very large number of modern Pagans do not necessarily possess any religious inspiration. That is to say, they have not become Pagan through an interest in witchcraft, or because they wish to learn Heathen divination methods. They have become Pagans because the Pagan respect for the natural world is the religious tradition that most agrees with an ecologically sound approach to the modern world.

Some Pagans are embarrassed by these associations, unwilling to draw lines of contact between themselves and the ecological protest movement. Others think of environmentalism as a fad, a short-lived experiment in branding that allows companies to charge us more money for less-efficient washing powder for a while. However, although the television no longer sells us 'dolphin-friendly' tuna, the dolphins still need saving.

It is important for more conservative Pagans to acknowledge their brethren in the ecology movement, not only for the sake of acceptance and harmony, but because one of the reasons the environmentalists are still ignored is that many media pundits try to associate them with callow youths. Until we see more mothers with children, pensioners with their dogs and businessmen in suits walking on protest marches, they will continue to imply that only unemployed travellers, lonely anarchists and bored students are interested in stopping road-building and other schemes.

There are many issues on which Pagans and environmentalists agree, but since many of the latter are secular, they sometimes act in ways which some would argue is in contradiction of the Rede. In Britain, we have become used to the sights of environmental protesters on television. Road-building schemes are blocked by tunnels, and fox hunts are thwarted by hunt saboteurs who block the horses' paths and lead the dogs on false trails. In America, the environmental protest movement can take an even more 'hands-on' approach. Some hardline environmentalists take part in 'monkey-wrenching', the deliberate interference in environmental exploitation which, as the name implies, involves throwing many a spanner in the works. This does not just mean boycotting the products of unsound companies, but it may also involve changing signs to mislead tourists, interfering with traps set by hunters, and sticking spikes in trees to damage sawmills. Even within the environmental movement itself, these actions have led to a heated debate. Some have argued that such direct action is the only way to counteract the murder of the environment, whereas others are concerned with the possible damage to innocent people. As a Pagan environmentalist, how can you countenance tree-spiking if it may lead to flying pieces of sharp machinery in a mill? Not only is the machinery damaged, but the operator could also be hurt and how does that fit in with 'harming none'?

Even the editors of the monkeywrenchers' bible, *Ecodefense*, remind protestors that action should only be considered as a last resort, after asking the questions: Who is my audience? What is my message? Will this deter destruction? Are there legal means not yet used? The question of what kind of action you take has as many answers as there are Pagans. Environmentally active Pagans protest about the destruction of forests because they are forced to watch areas of great natural beauty slowly killed by the concerns of distant businessmen. A road link that caused a great deal of strife in east London in the 1990s served very little purpose. Trees were cut down and people were evicted from their homes, and all so a sales representative heading for Cambridge could get out of London seven minutes faster. But sometimes it is necessary to see the forest for the trees. An apple that falls from a tree does not kill it. A tree that falls in the wood does not kill the forest. It is the forest that has the soul, not just the individual parts of it.

We do not all have the same power in society, but we do have the power to vote with our wallets, and to avoid products which do not conform to environmental principles. However, it is important to keep matters in perspective; the world is the way it is and most Pagans do not really want to return to prehistoric subsistence farming. Paganism does not have a principle of 'returning to the land', because that would be foolish. Where would the 'decivilizing' stop? The Pagan future is not an Amish-like society, stuck in an artificially determined past of self-contradictory stipulations. We hope we will never see silly arguments against the wise rubber cart wheels but in favour of carts, or the many ridiculous schisms that have rent these reclusive sects over such things as whether or not buttons and zippers are against the will of God.

By all means, fight against the rape of the natural world, and decide where you will draw the line and take your stand. But also remember that when you are ill, you have penicillin, when you wish to see your relatives, you can fly, and when you are hungry, you can buy food. Our ancestors did not have these facilities but they may well have leaped at the chance to use them if they had. Modern Paganism is not a negative reaction to modern technology, it is an attempt to ensure that it is used positively. If this book had been written on parchment, it would have done a lot more damage to the environment than it has, being composed in the paperless insides of a computer and printed on paper from renewable resources. We hope it is proving worth the hours you worked for the money to buy it, or the trip you made to borrow it, but if it is not, it can be shredded, pulped and turned into something else.

There is a difference between subsistence – those things you need to nourish your body, mind and spirit – and indulgence, or consumption for the sake of it. As with all Pagan matters, it is between you and your own conscience, but some decision on the subject is a good idea, since Paganism is centrally concerned with Mother Earth.

7   Celebrating the Festivals

As is the case with all religions Paganism has an annual pattern of celebrations which has developed from ancient roots, part of which has been recreated to fit modern needs and part of which has been Christianized or survived as folklore. The idea of celebrating eight festivals seems to have originated with the modern Druids, and Gerald Gardner probably lifted the tradition from them via his friend Ross Nicholls, who was head of one of the more Pagan of the Druid orders. Gardner, with his love of archaisms, called them 'sabbats', a word which featured in the seventeenth-century witch trials. There are four astronomical festivals – the two solstices of winter and summer and the two equinoxes of spring and autumn – plus the four main Celtic celebrations, which have been allotted arbitrary dates. Any calendar will give the times of the astronomical seasons, but in a period without clocks it would have been difficult to tell which day in particular was the longest, the shortest or the most equal in length. For this reason, the ancients probably began celebrating these festivals at the nearest full moon, rather than on the exact day, which we can now measure with modern technology. You should celebrate when it feels right, not because someone has written in a book somewhere that Candlemas absolutely *has* to be celebrated on 2 February. Why not watch for the first snowdrops to appear in your garden and then honour them as harbingers of spring? After all, people in the southern hemisphere have had to reverse the European cycle to accommodate their own seasons. If Australian Pagans can worship spring a full six months later than British Pagans, what difference will a few days make? As always, it is the thought that counts.

The idea of celebrating and marking the seasonal changes is common to all Pagan traditions worldwide, and dates from the times when the life of the tribe was dependent on the agricultural year and tied to the life and death cycles of the God figure. The Goddess figure never dies, but annually goes through her triple cycle from maid to mother to crone, whereas the God must die in the autumn, to be reborn again at Yule or late winter. The cycle of dying and resurrected gods of vegetation was a common feature of most ancient belief patterns, and was connected with the waning and waxing power of the sun and the reappearance of vegetation each spring. Naturally, this cycle was of vital interest to our ancestors, and even survives today in the New Year imagery of the venerable Old Year handing over the hourglass to a new-born baby. Modern Pagans who worship Nature can easily identify with the seasonal changes as that brings them closer to the land they treasure.

The cyclical festivals of birth and death are more than a mere celebration of an agricultural lifestyle, however. They serve to remind us of our own mortality, and of the passing of time. Each New Year is another year gone in our lives, and another chance to think over what we have done and how we might make things better. Each New Year can also be a new beginning, and the tradition still survives of making resolutions as we leave the winter solstice behind and the days start to get longer again. The difference is that, if you are a Pagan, there are eight different opportunities to take stock of your life and coax yourself into being a better person.

You do not have to be an initiate of a Wiccan coven or even a member of a group at all to celebrate the festivals. Recently there has been a tendency for local Pagans to get together to organize such celebrations for all comers. It is, after all, one of the nicest ways of convincing your local community that far from being evil Satanists you are actually just like them. Not only that, but many of the festivals they assume to be 'theirs' are actually yours.

The summer solstice celebration at Stonehenge, which was long associated with the Druids, was a magnet for hippies, Pagans and travellers until it was banned by the authorities in 1985. The limited access allowed in 1998 permitted some people on to the site, but they had to have passes. Although some Pagans have claimed that this is an unfair infringement of their rights, it is perhaps worth pointing out that whoever built Stonehenge probably did not allow all and sundry to swarm all over it either. True, the Government does not really have any claim to the site, but then, as we said in Chapter 3, nor do the Druids. Recently however, a group of Druids calling themselves the Gorsedd Bards of Caer Abiri began openly celebrating the festivals at the stone circle at Avebury.

There are no rituals cast in stone, as it were; the ones that follow are offered as examples that can be adapted to suit different circumstances or denominations. They are relatively simple in terms of trappings and can be worked anywhere, either alone or in company. Above all, remember that Paganism is a merry religion and there is no need to be po-faced and solemn about it. So why not dress up, have a good time, feast and make merry with friends or family, and get the children involved? They love a celebration.

If you have a suitable place and are prepared to brave the elements in winter, it is always worthwhile to celebrate out of doors, as Paganism is all about Nature, and you do not need fancy robes and a lot of grand ceremonial. If you prefer indoor working, all the rituals assume that the participants have bathed and are robed, and that some formal ritual of creating or opening a sacred space has been performed. Again, however, that is not essential, especially if you have friends in attendance who are not normally part of your hearth. There is no need to complicate matters.

A lot is left to the imaginations and creative abilities of the participants, and you can always mix and match with other published rituals or material you have devised yourselves. We give no advice about music, as that is far too individual a subject, but as long as you can find something suitable for all the participants, it is an excellent adjunct to any celebratory occasion, either during it or afterwards.

Samhain

This is properly pronounced 'sow-ain', although many modern Pagans prefer to say it as it is written. It is a late autumn festival which represented the temporary departure of the sun, and thus emphasized the departure of the God and his transformation into the Lord of the Underworld, while at the same time the Goddess became the crone, the old wise widow who conducts the dead to the Summerlands, the Celtic paradise. But if it was the festival of the dead, it was also the Celtic New Year, as death is but transitory before resurrection in spring to new life and new growth. It is traditionally celebrated on 31 October, which was Christianized as the Eve of All Hallows (or Hallowe'en), which has exactly the same emphasis on the souls of the departed. It falls in the Celtic month of Yew, a tree traditionally planted in churchyards. All Hallows is an important day in Roman Catholic countries in Continental

Europe, where Pagan trappings still survive in the German custom of lighting candles on family graves the night before, and the French tradition of placing pots of chrysanthemums in cemeteries. The Celts believed that at this time of the year the veil between the living and the dead was at its thinnest, and the same applies in other folk traditions. Apart from the esoteric religious significance of Samhain, however, it was also the time when the cattle were brought in from the pastures and all except the breeding stock were slaughtered and salted down for the months ahead. A bad year meant starvation at the end of winter, so our ancestors celebrated with a great festival of roasted meat to set themselves up with full bellies.

In modern times, Hallowe'en has become associated with parties, dressing up as witches and telling ghost stories, pursuits in which many Christians will happily indulge. The more fanatical, however, rail against such matters and publish dire warnings about 'dabbling with the occult', to such an extent that the Pagan Federation has produced a schools information pack which states, among other things: 'We believe that remembering the dead is no more sinister than Remembrance Day, and that children should be allowed to confront the concept of death in a safe way, just as they do by watching slightly scary television programmes.' This is a sombre time of the year, conducive to introspection, when the nights are long, the trees are almost bare of leaves, and the days are damp and dark.

For the ritual you will need a ceramic bowl with a dark-coloured interior, filled with fresh, clean water and placed in the centre of your sacred space. Bottled still mineral water is suitable. Decorate your altar with anything you can find outside, such as russet-coloured leaves, nuts, acorns, and an apple for each worshipper present. As a part of your opening ritual, you can invoke the goddess in her crone aspect, for the earth of the field is now bare without the God of the corn. Visualize her as an old woman clad in a long black garment, but as you gaze into her lined face you will see that her eyes are aglow with life, for she never dies.

All things must wither and die for so it is ordained. But thou, Lady of the Night Skies, I do entreat thee to be here with me/us tonight, and to be my/our guide through the long, dark months ahead. Help us to remember with love and delight those of our loved ones who have gone before us, and may you show us things we must know.

Then sit quietly and remember anyone who was particularly dear to you, and imagine them as they were, full of laughter and delight. Bid them come to your temple for a brief moment to share your rite. Do not be sad but rather give thanks in your heart for the fond moment you spent with parents, family and friends who have moved on to other realms. When you feel ready, say aloud:

In death there is life, and at the end of life is death, for the wheel is always turning. As the dark times draw nigh, the light of life is only dimmed, and it shall burst forth again. In the darkness when it is our time, we shall meet, and know and remember our loved ones again.

Go to the centre and sit by the bowl of water. Gaze steadily into it, not forcing yourself but drifting into a slight trance state. You may see visions, moving pictures and still images in the still surface of the water that will have a special meaning for you.

After the introspection, it is time to celebrate life. Consecrate the wine in the chalice and, holding it up to the candlelight, say:

This is the cauldron of rebirth. Let this wine be consecrated to life so that as I/we drink it I/we shall be renewed.

Then hold your hands palms down over the apples and concentrate on them feeling your life energy passing into them. Apples are sacred to the Goddess and are said to contain the seeds of knowledge. We do not fear the serpent, and willingly take the fruit he offers. Drink the wine and eat the apple, reflecting at the same time upon what you wish to change, both in your life and in the world outside it.

Yule (Winter Solstice)

Technically speaking, Yule is a Nordic term for the winter solstice, but it sounds better than Christmas! Most of the trappings we traditionally associate with the season are Pagan anyway – mistletoe, holly, indoor trees and the Yule log – but would seem to be Germanic in origin rather than Celtic. Where the Celtic year begins at Samhain, those groups with a Norse pantheon or origin are more likely to celebrate New Year at this time. Although the actual moment of the solstice differs from year to year, Pagans normally celebrate on the eve of 21 December, opening their presents as well as working a ritual.

The winter solstice marks the turning point in the year when the days become longer and there is a promise of spring to come. All the Pagan traditions celebrate it in some ways, as it is bound up with the life/death cycle of the God, and the Goddess in her darkest aspect. It is when she gives birth to the divine child/son/lover, whom she conceived in spring and who will now reign throughout the coming year.

It was only in AD 273 that the birth of Jesus was fixed by the Church as 25 December. Other estimates of his birthdate vary from late spring to early autumn! However, the 'traditional' date of Christmas was a cunning ploy by the early Christians to bring their spiritual leader in line with other solar deities, such as Shiva, Mithras, Dionysus and the Sun Unconquered. It gave the followers of Jesus an excuse to have a good time along with the Pagans, although in modern times, they give the impression that *we* are somehow usurping *their* festival. In Egypt, the dismembered and reassembled Osiris was buried on 21 December, and Isis gave birth to Horus, her son/lover, two days later. Mary in the stable was fulfilling her role as the Goddess/mother of the Christian tradition's own divine child, and the nativity legend is one of promise and light for the future. Above all, Yule is about having a good time, feasting, giving presents and sharing the good cheer with others who may be lonely or in need. But if you have children, there is no need for them to be deprived of the joy of the old man in a white beard bringing them gifts. Get a friend to dress up and call them Father or Mother Mistletoe, or something similar.

This is also an ideal time to involve children in the preparations. Decorate the house with greenery and garlands. Get hold of a nice big log if you have an open fire, and decorate it with ribbons and sprigs of holly to make it ready for burning on solstice night. You could even have a crib – a basket with a doll placed in a suitable position, to make a bed for the child who is to come, decorated with silver tinsel and a lighted candle. Children love the symbolism of the crib, and Pagans should have one too, based on their own myths. As part of the ritual, the doll can be crowned by a foil crown, or dressed in a robe, whatever takes your fancy. Have a fir tree, preferably with roots so that it can be replanted afterwards, with bright decorations and lights. If you have a window facing the street, put a large, red, unlit candle on the sill. Place two tall red candles on your altar and bank up the fire ready for the Yule log. For afterwards, prepare a feast of pudding and mince pies, mulled wine and other goodies. As all the candles will be blown out at one stage, have matches ready to relight them. Place an extra red candle in the east. As usual, have wine in the cup, bread or biscuits and anything else you think you may require. When everybody is ready and seated in the sacred space, the celebrant says:

> Our Lord the Sun, who warmed us in summer and gave life to the land that we should not starve, is now but a feeble flicker of light which must be extinguished this night, for so it is ordained. But in the darkness where she dwells, Our Lady, the Mother of All, awaits the birth of her son, the new light she has promised to us all, and who shall reign over the coming year in his splendour. As the God must finally die, so must the light die with him, for out of the darkness comes forth the promise of new life to come.

Extinguish all the lights, starting with the tree and then the quarter candles in reverse order (anticlockwise) and finally the altar candles. Sit in the darkness for a while, meditating about the mystery of rebirth. Women who have had children can remember their own labour, when they themselves took on the role of Goddess/mother.

The celebrant takes the matches and lights the new candle in the east, saying:

> In the east the sun is born, the flame of hope that shall lead us forth from the darkness into the light of the coming year. In her dark realm beneath the earth, the Goddess has heard our prayer, and we hear the cry of the new-born child in the stillness of the night. He is with us, weak and tiny, and let us wrap him warmly in the softest clothes. Let us present our gifts before him in worship and give him the love that lies in our hearts.

Relight the quarter candles clockwise, the altar candles and the tree. If there is a crib, now this is the time to crown the babe, robe it and offer gifts, a task for any children present, who can give things they have made. When that has been done, the celebrant says:

> So shall he grow to manhood strong and bold, ready to greet our Lady when she returns to be with us on earth. Let his mighty sword breathe life into the sacred Grail of immortality.

> Let him be crowned as the bold stag on the hill, the Lord of
> the forest and of the animals, and may his rays brighten our
> lives in joy and abundance through this coming year.

The next part of the ritual could be delegated to any child of sufficient
age or performed by an adult. White-robed, he or she should take one
of the altar candles, go to the candle in the window and light it, accompanied by everyone else. The following invocation should be spoken,
preferably learned by heart:

> In this time of joy we kindle this light as a symbol of the
> rebirth of the sun within our hearts. O Goddess, Mother and
> protector of the lonely and sad, may all those who pass by see
> it as the sign of hope and may there be love, joy, comfort and
> warmth kindled too in their hearts.

Return to the altar and consecrate or bless the cup and food, sharing
the communion. A toast should be drunk to all Pagan folk wherever they
may be, that their Yule will be blessed with warmth, love and light.
Then, close down the working area as usual, and make the offering to
the Earth, before the feast and the opening of presents begins. In Poland
it is customary to lay an extra place at the Yule table, and any stranger
who comes to the door will be invited to share the food.

Imbolc (Candlemas)

Imbolc literally means 'belly', and the name signifies the quickening of
life in the womb of the Earth Mother. It is a fire festival, with the emphasis on the light that will pierce the gloom of winter to herald the coming
of spring. It is also the festival of the Goddess mother figure worshipped
by the Celtic peoples as Bride (pronounced 'Breed'), who became
Christianized as St Brigit. Wells, in particular, are sacred to her, and if
you have one nearby, visit it and leave a gift by dropping in a coin or
tying a bright ribbon in a nearby tree. It is usually celebrated on 2
February, although St Brigit's Day is 31 January. In Rome, the month of
February was a time of purification, and the idea has been handed down
in the ritual of spring cleaning. Some Wiccans believe that at Imbolc, the
remnants of all Yule evergreen decorations must be burned, a symbolic
cleansing of what is past and preparing for the new, fresh life to come.

This festival is a special time for initiations, signifying as it does a new beginning, and even a non-initiate can use Imbolc as an excuse to renew old commitments or make fresh ones. One good idea is to keep a vigil through the night and go outside to see the sun rise and greet the Lord with a prayer. In practical terms, you could spring-clean the house and throw out or give away any unwanted objects. An attractive Irish custom is to make St Brigit's crosses – equal-armed Celtic crosses traditionally woven out of rushes. You could make one and hang it in your temple, or on the front door to welcome visitors. It should be burnt the following Imbolc, thus banishing all that was unwanted in your life the previous year.

It is an ancient Scottish tradition to prepare Bride's Bed, ready for her to enter the house during the night, and we have based this ritual around this practice, as it is a very evocative working, suitable for a lone practitioner as well as for a group. To prepare the bed, you can use the same basket and doll as you did at Yule, but this time it is a bed for the Goddess, so do not stint with any bits of material you may have. Line it with silk, satin or the finest velvet, and if you have children let them make a special coverlet and a pillow filled with sweet herbs. Dress the doll as finely as you can, and cover her head with a veil, as in her annual cycle she is just a maiden teenager at Imbolc. When the bed is ready, put it in your temple area and surround it with seven new, white, unlit candles. You will also need a broomstick or a bundle of twig, which should technically be cut from the rowan tree, as it is the month of Rowan in the tree calendar. Everyone in the temple should bring with them a gift for the Goddess: a crystal, for example, something they have carved, a piece of jewellery or even a snowdrop from the garden.

The celebrant should speak the following invocation to the deities as part of the opening ritual:

Gentle sweet Brighid, maiden of the coming spring, you who shine in the night sky ever bright and are returning to us from the dark places, I bid you come when I call to this temple and to dwell awhile with us in peace and love. I call too upon the young Forest Lord, growing through boyhood in the wild places. Soon thy Lady will await thee to greet thee in thy manhood, to be joined with the beauty of her womanhood.

When the opening rite has been completed and the sacred space created, speak the following prayer:

Now is the time when the sun begins again to burn brighter with renewed strength. Winter is passing and the days grow longer, as hope rekindles in our hearts. Let us take health and strength from his fiery splendour as we watch the renewal of life in this beautiful land. Let us sweep away old worries and feelings of darkness. Let us discard that pain and anger that may lie deep in our hearts, so that we too may be renewed as we await the spring. May the gentle light of our Mother, the Earth, enter into us, bringing new life and fresh vigour. Thus we sweep away the old and cleanse this place for welcoming in the new.

Take the broom or twigs and sweep your sacred space, moving anti-clockwise, banishing unwanted deeds, thoughts and feelings. As you do so, you could repeat the following chant:

Thus we banish winter, thus we welcome spring,
Say farewell to what is dead and greet each living thing.

After the ritual cleansing, sit for a while and meditate on the things that you have banished, and make yourself ready to take the young Goddess to your heart. When you are ready, light the candles around the bed, saying:

Let light there be, burning bright
To welcome Bride this sacred night.

You, or perhaps an older girl-child can now go to a door or window and open it, taking with you the altar candle or a candle lantern if you have one. As you look out, visualize the maiden goddess in the stars, shimmering with beautiful silvery light and dressed in white and blue. Call to her, bidding her enter your temple. Any others present should be standing behind you as you say:

Bride come, your bed is made, Bride come . . .

You will feel her enter, perhaps as a gentle breath of cool wind. Close the door or window and return to your sacred space. Kneel by the bed, present your gifts to the Goddess, speaking a dedication in your own words and offer any resolutions you have made for the coming months.

Finally, consecrate the wine and bread to share, and drink a toast to all good Pagan folk everywhere, who will also be celebrating the festival.

Ostara (Spring Equinox)

At Ostara the days and nights become of equal length. It is usually celebrated on 21 March, although an astronomical calendar will give the actual date of the equinox. The timing can be a little arbitrary, however, as spring may come earlier or later to the place where you live, and you may prefer to celebrate the rite when the flourishing garden tells you to. This is the time of the year when everything is bursting into leaf and when the young God is clad in his freshest greenery as he re-enters his kingdom. There he will meet his maiden bride and be reunited with her to restart the cycle of life. It is a time for us to celebrate. Our word 'Easter', the time when the Christians mourn the death and celebrate the resurrection of their saviour, comes from Oestre, a Nordic goddess whose symbol is the egg which holds within it the seed of a new life.

For this celebration, you will need a sword, wand, or similar symbol of maleness and bowl of hard-boiled eggs, which should be genuine free-range rather than laid in the obscenity of a battery house. You or your children can decorate them with brightly coloured dyes. You will also need an earthenware flower pot full of good earth, seven seeds of yellow or orange flowers (marigolds or sunflowers would be suitable) and some mineral water.

As an opening invocation, you could use the following words:

> I invoke thee, O Lady, Queen of the silver moon, virgin huntress of the wood, white as snow, unknowable and divine, to be with us in our rite that we may do thee honour and gaze upon thy beauty. I invoke, too, thy consort, the horned one of the wild places, splendid in manhood and power. Come on thy silent feet and be with us in our hearts this night. By seed and root, by bud and stem, by leaf and flower and fruit, by life and love, I invoke thee and call on thee.

All those present should sit and meditate upon the spring season as the Goddess and the God prepare for their sacred wedding that is not yet consummated. Then the celebrant should speak the following prayer:

O Great Mother, thou who art within me, I do feel thy presence long after the deep sleep of winter. Thou hast returned to the realms of earth and this blessed land. Thou hast brought the freshness of spring into the land, and rejoicing to its people. Stay now and dwell with us in thy fruitfulness and give peace, love and happiness to all who shall come here.

And the Lord of the Forest said: 'O Lady, I too have returned from the long winter hunt, and now do seek thee in the leafy glades of the fresh woodlands. In the darkness I was alone, but now in the light of thy love, I do honour and worship thee.'

The celebrant takes up the pot of earth.

Blessed is the Grail, the fountain from which we all spring, the centre of the circle, the origin of all things. In thee, this earth, dwells the living soul of this land. Enclose it within thyself to form the bed from which fresh life shall spring, as from the womb. And in the fullness of time, bring it forth in beauty.

The celebrant then places the tips of the fingers on the sword, saying:

As the sword is to the male, so the Grail is to the female. Conjoined they bring blessedness. Let this creature of earth be purified and consecrated, prepared to receive the seed, to nourish it and give it life.

If the celebrant is alone, he or she then plants the seven seeds in the pot and sprinkles them with water. If others are present, all should share in the planting. Then the celebrant says:

May this pure water pass into the earth. Swell the seeds, causing them to burst open, and help the young shoots strive upwards towards the air, where they shall be nurtured by the fire of the sun.

The celebrant than takes the pot and presents it to each quarter in turn. Holding it up to the north in front of the altar, she or he says:

As the male plants the seed in the female, who cherishes it in her womb, and in due time gives birth, so may this sacred earth harbour and nourish these seeds. O thou eternal sun, shine down upon this symbol of nature itself, bless it with thy warmth, that the seeds may grow and blossom. So too shall this land be fruitful. Bless my/our work here, that I/we may do honour to thee, and taking only what I/we need, share thy bounty with others.

After the planting ritual, take out the basket of eggs. Each person present should take one in the hand and breathe life into it, feeling it as a microcosm of the miracle of creation. Then the celebrant should bless the eggs, giving thanks for the blessings of new life, and afterwards they can be given to friends as presents. When the seeds have germinated and grown into young seedlings, plant them in the garden, in a window box or out in the wild.

Beltaine or Beltane

This great festival is celebrated on May Eve, 30 April or – ideally – at the nearest full moon. Weather permitting, it should be worked out of doors, around a bonfire on a hilltop, but if you have to work indoors, a candle in the centre of your space will have to do as a substitute. It is an old tradition to jump over the embers of a fire to bring luck and be cleansed and purified. It is a wonderful experience to stay up all night and greet the rising sun on May morning with friends. You can drum, sing, chant and feast to your hearts' content if you have access to a suitable spot. If you have a place that will remain undisturbed, say in a secluded garden, you can ritually plant some corn seeds to be cut down at Lughnasadh (see below).

Beltane is all about blossoming, fertility and the sacred union of Goddess and God, when the child of their bodies is conceived. In times past this union was celebrated as an act of sympathetic magic to ensure fertility for the coming year, and young couples would steal off into the woods to 'go a-Maying', as it was called. Naturally, the Church frowned on such licentious behaviour and did its best to desexualize the festival. The maypole, however, survived, though shorn of its power as a phallic symbol, as did the custom on May Day itself of bringing greenery into the church or house. As Pagans are unashamed of their sexuality, if you are in a loving relationship Beltane is a good time to make love as an offering to the earth. A ritual of marriage is outlined in Chapter 11, but that might be too formal a rite for Beltane, which is more of a time of merry lust and a healthy tribal rut. If you have a circle of friends you can dance the maypole in your temple if there is enough room. Get hold of a suitable pole and attach long, coloured ribbons to the top of it. A woman or child robed in white is chosen to stand in the centre and hold the pole while the others dance around, gradually enveloping her with their ribbons. There you have the symbolism of the Queen of the May, but if you are a woman and working solo, then you too are the Queen incarnate.

The above comments provide ideas for an outdoor celebration, but the following ritual assumes an indoor working for one person or a small group. You will need a fresh red or orange candle in the centre to symbolize your Bel-fire, and you should decorate your temple with plenty of flowers and fresh greenery. This is a festival of great joy, and the women and children should have flowers in their hair, while the men can have crowns of oak leaves. If you think it might be appropriate, why not celebrate your rite naked to emphasize the freedom from restraint in the Beltane myths?

After the formal opening, in which the celebrant can invoke the presence of the God and Goddess as bride and groom, he or she goes to the centre and lights the candle, saying:

> Thus I light the Bel-fire bright
> In this place that it may give us light.
> As we dance and make merry in our rite
> May we blessed be this night.

You and any others present should dance clockwise around the candle, gradually speeding up to raise the power. Imagine you are dancing naked on fresh green grass in a wooded grove with the full moon bright above you. As you dance, chant:

> Round and round the fire we run,
> God and Goddess joined as one.

When the celebrant feels ready, he or she should shout 'Stop!', and all present should kneel and place their hands on the floor, letting the power from the dance flow down their arms into the earth, visualizing it as a stream of light giving fertility to the Mother. Then sit in a circle, quietly meditating in the candlelight about the sacred union, which in reality is the joining of opposites to create the cosmic balance or polarity. Do not be ashamed to feel your own sexuality, and if you are a couple, you could decide to make love in the temple at this point. Otherwise, you can consecrate the chalice as a symbol of the sacred marriage, using your knife or wand if you have one. If there are a man and woman, the man traditionally kneels and holds the cup for the woman to bless, which she does by lowering the tip of the knife or wand into the wine, pulling light in through the crown of her head and letting it flow down the shaft into the cup. As she does so, she says:

> As the sword is the male, so the cup is the female, the cup from which we all sprang. In their union lies blessedness, for there is no part of us that is not of the gods.

Then drink the wine and share the food. When you have finished, take the last drops and a piece of the bread outside into the garden, if you have one, and there, under the moon, offer them to the Earth.

Litha (Summer Solstice)

This festival takes place on or around 21 June, and marks the time when the days are longest and the sun God is at the height of his powers, but afterwards starts his steady decline. We know next to nothing about Stone Age ritual or religion, but we do know that their monuments (including Stonehenge) were oriented towards the sunrise at midsummer solstice. It must therefore have been important to those early people who were without reliable calendars. This was long before the Druids who, as we saw in Chapter 3, worshipped in natural places, not stone temples. So modern Druid groups have no historical connection with Stonehenge, although that is no reason why they should not perform their rites there. The hippie festival which started there during the early 1970s (and was finally banned in 1984) came about by accident, and was originally a very small affair. They sang and drummed all night, waiting for the sunrise over the Hele Stone. Afterwards, children were named and marriages celebrated, all of which was part of the revival of Pagan worship in Britain.

In one of the traditional God Cycles, the Oak King, the ruler of the waxing year, having reached the height of his powers, is symbolically slain by his replacement, the Holly King, ruler of the waning year, who in turn is slain at Yule. The Christians echo this with the legend that John the Baptist was supposedly beheaded on 24 June, and all over Europe people light so-called St John's Fires on hilltops.

The solstice is a fire festival, and a celebration of the harvest that is to come. As far as the Goddess is concerned, she is at the height of her fecundity, pregnant with the mystical child she will bear at Yule. She blesses the growing crops as well as the harvest of fruits, which is in progress at that time. Modern Pagans like to work out of doors, and may sit up through the night in order to greet the dawn with a prayer of renewal. They keep a fire burning all night, although that is somewhat impractical if you live in a town and only have a small garden.

We think that the solstice is a good time to explain some basic astronomy to a child who is old enough, such as the phases of the moon, and why the days become shorter or longer. There are a number of ways of celebrating with children. You can simply work indoors in the evening before, or set the alarm for just before dawn and go outside to greet the rising sun. In addition, you can go outside at midday on the actual solstice and greet the sun with a prayer for harvest. The following is a suggestion for a simple ritual for the evening before or the solstice day itself.

Prepare a red candle on your altar, to symbolize the bonfire and the power of the sun, together with a bouquet and a bowl of water. You could make a fresh fruit salad, to eat afterwards, and any children can make their own chaplets of flowers. Decorate your temple space with lots of fresh flowers, as the solstice is a time of fulfilment and joy. As you open the sacred space, say:

> Greetings, mighty Lord of the sun, ruler of the midsummer skies. You are at the height of your powers and the earth rejoices at the warmth and life you bring. The woods are decked in your green cloak and in your orchards and fields the promise of your harvest is being fulfilled. Your creatures, too, are bringing forth their young to enrich your realm. We, the children of the sun, give thanks for your warmth and light, for the pleasures of summer, for the long days and the star-sparkling nights. We bid you welcome and may this our temple be filled with warmth and light, that we may do you honour. Greetings, too, Lady of the ripening fields, hail and welcome. As the fruit of your womb quickens, we offer you our worship and our praise, thanking you for the promise of

fulfilment. May we, your children, also find fulfilment in the days to come.

Light the red candle and sit quietly, looking into the flame, thinking about the summer and the light of the sun. If there are children present, talk to them about the changing seasons and how the God is born, dies away and is born again each year, year after year. Meditate for a while about trees laden with fruit, and corn fields ripening in the sunlight. Imagine the Goddess as a fecund, pregnant woman in a setting of fields and orchards, soaking up the sun into her belly. Then get up and dance clockwise around the altar, perhaps chanting:

> Dance around the fiery flame.
> The Lord of Life is come again
> To bless this earth and give it birth,
> Though he himself must wane.

Do this seven times, then take the bowl of water, explaining that it represents the water of life and the cauldron of rebirth. Just as nature needs the strength of the sun, it also needs the nourishment of water, the gift of the Goddess. There can never be one without the other. Sprinkle yourself and any others present with a few drops, and say a prayer that you may all be given the gift of intuition and the knowledge of life. Then take the bowl, walk out into the garden and ritually sprinkle the flowers with drops of the water. If you do not have a garden, then a potted plant can be used in its place. The final act is to consecrate the wine and enjoy yourself, alone or with your friends.

If you have worked this ritual the evening before the solstice, go outside on the actual day and find a peaceful spot. Sit facing the midday sun, stretch out your arms and legs and invite the warmth to enter your body. As you do so, utter an invocation for strength and wish for any changes you want to make in your life. A particularly beautiful invocation comes from ancient Egypt and is ascribed to the pharaoh Akhnaten:

> Thy dawning is beautiful in the horizon of heaven
> O living Aten, beginning of life
> Thou fillest every land with thy beauty
> For thou are beautiful, great, glittering, high over the earth
> Thy rays, they encompass the lands, even all that thou hast
>   made

Thou art Ra, and thou hast carried them all away captive
Thou bindest them with thy love
Though thou art afar, thy rays are on the earth
Though thou art on high, thy footprints are the day.

Lugnasadh (or Lammas)

This festival is traditionally celebrated by Pagans on the evening of 31 July. Lugh was a corn God, possibly of Irish origin, who was worshipped throughout Celtic Britain and is an archetypal young god figure. Essentially, the festival is a celebration of the corn harvest, and in parts of Britain, the cutting of the last sheaf of corn is still an occasion for festivity. Corn dollies are also made at this time, and they are Pagan in origin. Lugnasadh was Christianized as Lammas, but their harvest festival services are but pale imitations of earlier rites. The Saxons celebrated the festival as Loaf Mass.

There are, however, deeper connotations. In the ancient world there were goddesses associated with corn (notably Ceres and Demeter) and the harvest was seen as the bounty of the womb of the Mother. It was a time of rejoicing, but it was also a time of sacrifice, either actual or symbolic. We see the Goddess in a triple aspect – maiden, mother and crone – who never dies but changes with the season. As we have seen, with the onset of winter, the Goddess enters her dark aspect, to emerge in the spring as the maiden, while the God *dies* every year, to be reborn. This ritual death probably began as a human sacrifice, perhaps of a criminal or prisoner of war. The ritual shedding of blood was bound up with the cutting of the last sheaf of corn, as the God of plenty breathed his last and the fearful farmers prayed that he would return with the following spring. The rites of harvest time are a mourning for Lugh as a sun god, whose light is inevitably beginning to wane. The old folk song 'John Barleycorn' is based around this myth, but you may also notice many similarities within the Christian eucharist.

Human sacrifice is both illegal and unfashionable these days, but there is an initiation rite in some Wiccan traditions, in which a man must face up to his secret fears of womanhood, also known as the Dark Lady. The candidate must go into the woods, where he encounters the priestess and is stripped naked by her women. The priestess then makes a small cut in his skin so that a small amount of blood flows into the earth, and then, as healer, she binds the wound to symbolize that even in death she is merciful.

Lugnasadh can be celebrated indoors or outdoors, and any working should revolve around giving thanks to the Earth Mother for her gifts. The essential symbolism is of home-baked bread, fresh foods in season, wine and flowers. If you can, try making your own corn dolly or buy one ready-made to hang in your house as a reminder of the corn harvest. You may already have a place where you planted corn in the spring, but if not, try to find a place, perhaps an ancient site, where you will not be disturbed. Invite your friends and get them to bring food to share, preferably something that they have either made themselves or bought fresh – fruit, for example. The whole ceremony is a harvest celebration as the sun starts his descent into the greater darkness and the Goddess prepares for her own symbolic journey into the underworld.

For the communion you will need some bread, which ideally you should have baked yourself in honour of the corn deities. If possible, light a fire in the centre of your space. Indoors, use a candle, and decorate the temple with seasonal fruits, greenery and bundles of corn. Whether indoors or not, you will need an ear of corn or a maize cob ready on the altar.

When you open your sacred space, make an invocation something like this:

Lady of the harvest, great Mother, whose promise is fulfilled each year to us as we honour your bounty, we entreat thy presence among us this day as we rejoice with all of nature. We entreat, too, the presence of the Lord of the harvest, and give thanks that even in death you will return to us as the seasons pass. May the shedding of your blood nourish the fair realms of the Lady, and may all the peoples on this earth have food in plenty.

Light the candle or place wood on your fire and sit for a while, quietly meditating on the problems of hunger in the Third World, praying silently for both peace and plenty for the victims of greed and war. This is a good time to talk to any children present about such matters as deforestation and pollution, or about refugees and others who do not have well-stocked shops and enough to eat. Afterwards, the celebrant can make the following declamation:

The time has now come when the summer's promise has blossomed in full bounty in this land of Earth. The fields have yielded up the golden corn, the vines are heavy and the land has blessed us with a bountiful harvest for the dark times ahead. Let us give thanks to the Lady of the earth, who has given of herself that we may have plenty when the warmth fades from our land. For the Lady says to us, the bounty of the earth is my gift to you, for my love is timeless. The harvest is freely given as is a mother's love to her children. The Lord of the forest filled me with his warmth as my fruits ripened and the corn swayed golden in the gentle summer winds. I am your Mother. From me comes the eternal cycle of love that never dies. Even as I age now, do not grieve, for although I will soon pass into the dark, I shall never leave you. During the long sleep of winter, I am she who spins at the centre of the web. Within my womb I bear the seed of the new season, ready to spring forth when light and life return to the land.

At this point, the celebrant takes the ear of corn and holds it aloft in offering to the deities. He or she then kisses it and passes it around to the others, who do likewise.

The seed of life was planted in my womb. Let it be nurtured and protected the dark winter long. Remember this my promise. I am with you always and the darkness will not sunder my love.

Those present should link hands and dance clockwise around the candle or the fire, chanting joyfully:

Lord and Lady, blessed be,
Thus we dance so fair and free
For the harvest rich and bright,
Before the fall of winter's night.

If you already have corn planted, the celebrant should take a sharp sickle or knife and cut it, saying:

Thus we take, but only according to our needs. Great Mother, we offer thanks for all the blessings that we have received, and we ask for strength in our work, that this our land will become a worthy temple to you, our Mother. May our love and our labour through the winter prepare us for the blessings of spring to come. We ask too for your power to descend on this planet Earth, despoiled by the greed of man. Let none desire more than their share of the Earth's riches. Let war and famine be banished and let all mankind return to the love of nature and the knowledge of your presence. Let all your children, the good Pagan folk, unite to work for peace and plenty. So shall it be.

Consecrate the wine and the bread, and take the communion in silent reverence. Harvest is a time for celebration, so share your food with others if possible, to laugh and sing, play games and enjoy the warmth of the gently fading sun. When it is time to close the sacred space if you have created one, say the following requiem for the departed Lord:

Our Lord lies bleeding upon the earth, cut down in order that we may live. We honour his sacrifice with our love, and weep no more tears. For we know that he will come again among us, his children, and we shall dance, feast and make merry in his honour. His pain is the pain felt by all living things that must die and pass into the darkness, but he departs to the realm of the Dark Lady, who will heal his wounds and in due time bring him forth as her promise to us. Hail and farewell.

Mabon (Autumn Equinox)

As Lugnasadh marks the start of harvest, so the equinox on or around 21 September marks its end. The remaining products are gathered in and the natural world prepares for the long sleep of winter. Day and night are again equal in the perfect balance of nature, and for Pagans this can be considered a time for summing up our own sense of balance with our lives. Is there anything about ourselves that is top-heavy, and causing us to lean too far one way or the other? Are we too dependent on any one person or thing, for example? Let us try and keep ourselves as balanced as the day and night of the equinox. For those of us in a relationship, this is a good time to remind ourselves that love is a two-way street. If we are relying on our spouse, can they equally rely on us for love and support?

In practical terms you can make necklaces of seeds and nuts for yourself, your children and friends. As an alternative or addition to a rite in your temple, why not invite your friends to a meal in the form of the traditional harvest supper? Decorate your dining area with autumn leaves, fruit, nuts and dried flowers to give as festive an air as possible. Invite any members of your hearth to the feast, or friends who are sympathetic to your beliefs. Ask them to wear a robe of similar loose clothing, for this is more than a simple excuse for overindulgence. The meal will be a ritual of thanksgiving in itself, especially if it is prepared from fresh produce with love and reverence, instead of being grabbed from the frozen food section of the local supermarket. Your table will become your magic circle or sacred space for the evening, and all those present will be blessed by good food and merry company.

Place on the table in front of the host or hostess's seat a bottle or decanter of drink and a plate of bread with enough pieces for each person present, plus a slice for the Earth offering to come later. As a more formal alternative, once seated, a white-robed child can bring them and place them in front of you. When everything is ready, and you and your guests are all seated at the table, say the following grace:

> We give thanks to the Lord and Lady for the bounty of the harvest, and may they bless this food, that we may be nourished.

Take the wine (or other drink) and hold it up in consecration, saying:

> I consecrate this wine, that it may refresh us and give us good cheer.

Then hold your hands palm down over the bread and say:

> I bless this bread, the food of life itself, that our hunger may be stilled. Grant, O Lord and Lady, that the hunger of all may be satisfied.

After the formal consecration, you should take the drink and serve the guests by filling their glasses, after which you should serve each with a piece of bread. When you are back in your place, raise your glass and offer a traditional toast:

> To the Old Ones and good folk wherever they may be.
> Merry meet, merry part and merry meet again.

Bon appetit! There is a great satisfaction in sharing food in merry company. When you have finished, do not forget the Earth offering before everyone departs.

If you have a garden, no matter how small, this is the time of year to clear out any dead foliage and cover vulnerable plants against the dangers of frost damage. Pile up the rubbish and have a good bonfire, which will enrich the earth with its valuable ash. As you do so, meditate about anything that you wish to clear out and burn from your own life so that you will be purified as well. Put on some warm clothing and construct a simple ritual around the bonfire with a dance and a chant of thanksgiving for the harvest if you are secluded enough not to bother your neighbours.

Working through a ritual year and celebrating the festivals, either alone or with friends, is an experience that will enrich your life enormously. It will give you an awareness of the seasons as they turn, and remind you of your place in the universe. You will find that you have become closer to the natural world as a result, as well as gaining an understanding of the death and rebirth cycles of the God, and the eternal transition of the Goddess from maid to crone. It is also a sobering thought that this year of life, death and life again is one of a paltry few in your existence on the Earth. Even if you live to a ripe old age, you are unlikely to see more than a hundred summers; the cycle of festivals in the year is designed to remind you that life itself can pass like a lazy summer's day. Enjoy the sunshine while you can, and love all.

There is no compulsion involved in Paganism, and even if you go to a public celebration rather than working in your hearth, you are at least doing something positive. Always remember that even if you are working alone, you are tuning into the great company of other Pagan folk who are keeping the festivals elsewhere. As you raise your chalice, bless them too as they will be blessing you.

8   The Magic of Nature

Many people are attracted to Paganism by the thought of magical power, and within the Wiccan tradition especially, will demand to be taught how to cast spells, place curses and conjure with magical forces. Pagans do indeed 'cast spells', but as we have pointed out elsewhere, so do Christians. The difference is in terminology, not in the forces at work – some Christians can heal by laying on hands, Christian congregations can influence events with the power of prayer, the power of a Christian service can send the audience out into the world with a warm glow and a smile, ready to do good deeds. And the act of praying, kneeling in a sacred space and opening oneself to God, is a simple but effective form of meditation. Pagans do all these things, in a slightly different manner admittedly, but with very similar aims and effects. If the way of Christian worship (or indeed, that of any other religious denomination) appeals to you and works for you, then you are unlikely to be reading this book. If you feel that these religions lack a certain something, that you prefer the practices and attitudes of Paganism, then perhaps that is a more appropriate way of attuning yourself to the divine.

Curses are theoretically possible in Paganism (just as Satanic black masses are theoretically possible as a reversal of Christian ceremony), but they break two golden rules of Paganism. If you were to curse someone, it would involve the channelling of negative energy – you would have to pray for hatred and harm, to wish evil upon another living creature. This is quite obviously in opposition to the Pagan law to 'do as you will, if it harm none', because you will clearly be harming someone. Furthermore, Wicca has a vague notion of karma, in that any deed you do will be magnified and returned to you threefold. Kindness shown to others will beget kindnesses towards you. A hand held out in friendship will find three hands waiting to take it. Teachers who teach well will learn much more from their students. But conversely, an act of evil or hatred against another human being will beget thrice again the negative energy upon yourself. Attack another person in any manner, and it will eventually impact on you, perhaps directly as your acts backfire, or indirectly as your conscience torments you with your deeds.

There are no rationalizations that will make such activities acceptable. If you have negative feelings towards someone, work them out in some way, but you are not a Pagan if you harm another human soul. Sometimes personalities may be incompatible and you may find antipathy welling up between two members in a group. If that is the case, then one or both of them has problems that need to be sorted out, either alone or by a meeting of the group. If you are the nominal leader of a group, perhaps you should reach out to the members separately in private. If matters become so heated that the group decides to cast out a member (see Chapter 11 for a banishing ritual), even this act should be undertaken without ill will. Do not stoop to the level of negativity, Paganism is a positive religion about growth. You should not stunt your spiritual growth by behaving like a spoilt child if you cannot get your own way.

The Colour of Magic

In the everyday world, people who have heard a little about Paganism may mention 'white' or 'black' magic. You may even have heard a Pagan priestess in the media describe herself as a 'white witch', as opposed to the supposedly nasty 'black' variety. These distinctions are not quite what they seem, and in fact much of the terminology has grown up through various attempts by modern Pagans to dissociate themselves from centuries of persecution and propaganda. The term 'white witch' is merely a short-hand attempt to remind non-Pagans that Pagans are inherently good, not wizened crones fiddling with unmentionable items in a cauldron and causing mischief.

Magic is neither black nor white; it is simply magic. Some Pagan denominations, especially those that rely on creative visualization or elemental ceremonies, may instead talk about a whole rainbow of different colours. White magic for rituals of cleansing and positivity, blue for healing and scrying, red for firing up your resolve or golden for suffusing your space with the energy of the sun. These colours are arbitrary; in your research you may find that they have different applications in different denominations. It may often depend on the tradition from which you draw your patron deities. Some may regard blue as the colour of the air element, others (such as the Order of Brighid) use green to represent water and blue to represent the sky. The geographical origin of your pantheon may determine the various roles of colours; different languages use colours in different ways. The Greek tradition has many shades of black but fewer shades of red, the Chinese has over a dozen reds, the Celtic recognizes many shades of grey and brown. The Chinese Pagan tradition uses black to represent water (the colour of impenetrable depths) and does not recognize air as an element at all – in feng shui and its associated disciplines, air is replaced by wood in the magical tradition. Furthermore, in the Chinese tradition, earth is yellow, because that is the colour of the silt that washes into the Yellow River. In short, there are no overriding rules about colour in magic. As long as you feel your choice of colours (or lack of them) works for you, then it will be fine.

Basic Magical Workings

If you are a relatively new Pagan, you may be working with a teacher, or have joined a hearth, coven or group that is already up and running and which is giving you some form of practical guidance or instruction towards gaining greater knowledge. Otherwise you will be on your own, either alone or with equally inexperienced friends, and this will mean that there are certain skills you will have to acquire.

The following suggestions are based on several recommendations to students, and are based on the practices of several different Pagan denominations. They can be worked by solo practitioners or a small hearth. If you are in the latter it is recommended that you get into the habit of regular meetings; you might consider celebrating the Feast of the Earth Mother (see Appendix 1) as a monthly communion rite. But one thing is essential: before you start anything, work out what it is you wish to achieve and why. We recommend at the very least that you write down a running order on a small card, and include such activities as 'healing for Tom's mother' and 'a card reading for Beth'. In that way, nothing will get forgotten.

Healing

There is one particular field in which many Pagans actively participate, and that is healing. On a practical level, this may mean obtaining knowledge about some of the disciplines of alternative therapy. Not all of these require years of training, although if you intend to set yourself up officially as a practitioner, it is sensible to acquire proper, recognized qualifications. But it is possible to study such methods as herbalism, crystal working, massage or aromatherapy at evening classes, by correspondence, at workshops or simply by reading about them, and it is a help to have at least a working knowledge of one or more of them. Whatever you do, however, tread gently and avoid overestimating your capabilities, as the New Age world is already full of therapists making dubious claims for their powers.

A good stock of general herbs and aromatherapy oils is a must in every Pagan household, and if you go out and pick your herbs yourself with love in your heart they will serve you well. The modern medical profession relies heavily on artificial healthcare measures, but the Pagan way encourages you to seek out the tried and traditional remedies that may already exist in nature. If you have a mechanical problem with your body then you will require the efforts of a surgeon, but in the case of a chest cold, why not try lungwort and coltsfoot before rushing down to the pharmacy?

Pagans can also be of great use in the field of spiritual healing, perhaps combined with some of the alternative disciplines mentioned above. Spiritual healing means the application of the powers of the mind and magic to effect or speed up someone's natural healing processes. There is nothing mysterious in this; we all have the latent power to heal, it is just more developed in some than in others. There are shelves full of books on the subject and you would do well to consult a few, although many are turgid in the extreme.

The following suggestions are based on personal experience, and are offered as a basis for individual experimentation. For example, some years ago, Anthony Kemp was suffering from a combination of work-related stress and jet lag, so he went to see a woman who was known to be a good healer. She gave him a bath containing essential oils, followed by a whole-body massage, and then passed a pendulum over his body to search for any areas of particular stress. She then applied her hands to places that she felt needed easing, and when she had finished, she gave him a cup of herbal tea. The result was that he promptly fell into a deep sleep and woke up a few hours later feeling 100 per cent better. The doctor would probably have done nothing more than prescribe a few pills.

Magical healing falls into two broad categories, the first being where the subject is present and the other where he or she is absent. To deal with the latter case first, imagine you know somebody who is in hospital. The first thing you can do on receiving the news is to light a candle. While some recommend blue as the colour of healing, others suggest that red, the colour of life blood, is more appropriate. In fact, the colour itself does not really matter, as it is the intention that counts. This can be done at any time without going through the rigmarole of bathing, robing and setting up your sacred space. It is a good idea to have a consecrated candle-holder permanently ready in your household shrine, and some spare candles handy in a drawer.

Take one out and hold it in the warmth of your hands while visualizing the person you wish to help. Imagine that person as you know him or her, full of life and energy, and as you do so take out the candle and light it. Then, gazing into the flame, project your own energy out to the patient as your gift. See that energy as a stream of warm, orange-coloured light flowing out from the centre of your forehead, the so-called third-eye chakra, and as you do so, try to visualize your friend lying in a hospital bed. Let your rays of light flow around him or her, and once you can hold that image in your mind, change the visualization to one of your friend as you would *like* him or her to be – walking in the countryside or sitting in a favourite pub for example. Finally, say a brief prayer to your deity, stating what you sincerely wish for your subject, and then leave the candle to burn out. This simple spell can work wonders, and only takes a few minutes on a busy day.

It is more difficult to do the same for somebody you do not know, perhaps a relative or acquaintance of a friend. The best policy is to ask for the name, age and physical description of the person, and try to weave these details as far as possible into the visualization.

The same techniques can be adapted in a ritual atmosphere, either alone or with friends. If you are on your own in your temple you can adapt the candle spell in a more formal way by consecrating the candle to the subject's name. You can do this by taking some consecrated anointing oil in the palm of your hand and gently rubbing it into the candle while softly chanting the name over and over again as you concentrate on the person. When you feel ready, place the candle in the holder, but before lighting it make an invocation to your favourite deity or one of the known healing gods or goddesses, such as the Egyptian Thoth or the Greek Hermes. You could say, for example:

> In this my sacred temple, I invoke thee, [Name], that thou mayest aid me to bring healing to [name of subject]. Lend me thy potency, that with my power of love and light I may relieve the pain and heal the body of [name of subject]. May he/she soon be well and filled with lightness and strength.

After the invocation, light the candle and start the visualization process by staring into the flame. If you are working for someone you do not know, it is a great help if you can get hold of a photograph. Working with a group I have found it effective to sit in a circle holding hands. After the invocation the participants visualize the healing ray entering their heads and running down their arms into the circle. The next step is to visualize it as a ring of light, which is then imagined as spinning clockwise, faster and faster as the group concentrates. As the tension builds up, everyone should visualize the subject until the person presiding feels that it is time to send the intention on its way by calling out:

> Let [name of subject] be healed!

The above working assumes that the subject is in a distant hospital bed, but the same techniques can be used to suit different purposes. Take, for example, someone you know who is in pain from arthritis of the hands, or perhaps chronic backache. First visualize the person, then concentrate on the area where the pain is most acute, focusing your ray there as you transmit it. In the case of mental disease, concentrate on the head. When you are working to heal yourself, concentrate the ray inside your own body rather than projecting it outwards. It is not only human beings who can benefit from healing, as the same applies to animals and even plants. If you have a favourite rose bush in the garden and it is looking a bit sad, give it some healing and it will perk up.

Inevitably, you will suffer disappointments on some occasions. Sometimes your healing will not work, and there may be valid reasons. If it is the karma of the subject to suffer illness, no amount of witchery will effect a cure, and every one of us will eventually die some time. If your subject has a broken leg, he or she will need an expert to set the fracture, and in such a case the intention should be to help the break to knit together healthily and free from pain. But there have been countless examples of people with cancer who have either cured themselves by ignoring the disease or been healed by the intervention of others. There is often a lot of 'mind over matter' in so-called miraculous cures, even in the supposed divine interventions of Lourdes. How much is the power of a deity, and how much the seeker's own will to be healed? If Pagans know a working is being performed, that knowledge itself can often have an effect; they get better because they *want* to believe in the effectiveness of the spell. We have ourselves had the experience of someone asking for a certain working to be performed, and then to ring back before we had started to thank us for our efforts. In such cases, it is best to say nothing and let them believe it was the spell you had not yet cast, for when you actually do get round to it on the next request, the effect will be doubled.

Healing with the subject present assumes a number of things: that the patient is in agreement and will allow you to perform your magical working; that she or he accepts your competence and that you yourself know what you are doing. At the very least, you and your patient should be in agreement that Paganism is a viable belief system. If one or both of you is just mumbling words you do not believe, you might as well read the phone book to each other for all the good it will do. Having said that, there is no reason not to try some healing if someone you know is unwell and trusts you. The healing power lies in your hands and we all have the ability to heal by touch at any time and in any place. Focus the healing ray in your hands and project it into the subject while exerting the will to smooth away the pain. Some writers on healing suggest that you should not actually touch the subject, but hold your hands an inch or two away from the body. There is no set method, and everyone must experiment to find what works best for them. This experimentation may take some time, and you may attempt a healing on a subject who is sitting in an armchair or in a formal ritual setting within your hearth. Ultimately, however, once you have trained your 'healing muscles' you will no more need a ritual than you need a pointy hat and a broomstick. The only caveat with healing is to learn before you leap, and be aware of your limitations and the moral issues involved.

A useful tool in any form of healing activity is the ability to see auras, which are the etheric 'other bodies' that surround all living entities like shrouds of coloured light. They can be photographed using a special technique called Kirlian photography, which was developed in Russia, but they can also be seen by the naked eye if you train yourself to look. All of us can sense the aura of another person, which may be the origin of the feeling of 'being watched'. It is not the visual aspect of the person but his or her aura which we subconsciously 'feel' with our own auric field. When people say, 'He sent shivers up my spine', it means they picked up the negative vibrations of the other person, resulting in a reaction of revulsion or fear. It also accounts for dislike of having strangers too close to us in the confines of a lift or on a crowded train; others intrude into our auric space, which extends to about a foot around each individual.

The best technique for developing the power to actually see auras is to place the subject with his or her back to a neutrally coloured wall or curtain and concentrate on a spot just to the left or right. If you hold your concentration you will see bands of colour gradually forming, and with practice you will be able to hold the image for quite some time. A healthy aura is bright and throbbing with energy, while an unhealthy one is dull and sluggish.

Dowsing

Another useful skill is pendulum dowsing, which not everyone can learn; we know a very well-trained and magical person who cannot get a twitch from a pendulum. The technique was first really explored by the archaeologist T.C. Lethbridge, whose work is neatly summed up by Colin Wilson in his book *Mysteries*. Lethbridge discovered that every object emits energy at a different rate, which can be picked up by holding a pendulum over it. Depending on its distance from the object, the pendulum will start to rotate or swing. This pendulum is a small weight, which can be made from anything, suspended from a piece of thin cord or even a jewellery chain. Some witches use the silver pentagram they wear around their necks, but you should experiment with several different 'tools', using natural materials, or even a plastic bead hung from a fishing line. It is not the material of the pendulum that acts as a transmitter/receiver but rather the actual energies involved between the operator and the object.

One experiment you can try is to take the cord of your pendulum between your finger and thumb and hold it with a cord length of about 8 inches over your right and left wrists alternately, with your palms facing upwards. You may find that the pendulum will rotate quite strongly, anticlockwise over your left wrist and clockwise over your right wrist. It seems to pick up the life energy in the veins that are near the surface. It might not happen, but could well work first time. Once you find that it does work, go on to conduct more experiments. Many people will say that the rotation could have been simply a chance movement of your fingers, or that you consciously influenced the swing of the pendulum, so see if you really are attuned to dowsing. Try it out on objects made from different metals, noting the ideal cord lengths in each case, and then enlist your friends' help. Wait outside the room while they hide things, and then see if the pendulum and your practice with it has made you a better seeker. Walk into the room, hold out the pendulum at arm's length, and visualize the object you are searching for. Move slowly from side to side, and if the pendulum twitches or moves in a certain direction it will tell you how close you are to the target. The way in which the pendulum rotates or swings may also indicate a line of sight, showing where to reposition yourself for a better view of the object you seek. The closer you move to the object, the faster the pendulum will rotate, until it is strongest when the object is directly beneath it. Using this method, Anthony Kemp once found a contact lens that had been dropped at a party into a thick pile bathroom carpet.

There is no space in a general book such as this to discuss dowsing in depth, but it is well worth exploring, not just for finding lost objects, but for determining the condition of unwell individuals. It is, for example, a useful diagnostic tool for detecting muscle stress. It can also be used for determining the sex of an unborn baby in the womb – it should rotate clockwise for a boy and anticlockwise for a girl.

Divination

Another very old technique used by Pagans is divination, which some may call fortune-telling, but which others take more seriously, just as many people distinguish between the conjuring and trickery that is 'magic' and the real harnessing of natural power that is 'magick'. Some Pagans regard 'fortune-telling' as charlatanry, waving 'magical' devices in front of people and then telling them what they want to hear. Divination, on the other hand, is entered into with the utmost seriousness.

Tarot cards are particularly popular divination tools, although there are many other methods. Like a magical ritual or the invocation of a deity, the cards themselves are relatively unimportant. They are the interface between your mind and the invisible spirit world. Who knows whether they open gateways to spirits who answer your questions, read the future, or simply focus your mind so that you can extrapolate and hazard a guess about the future from whatever position you find yourself in? Anyone can go out and buy a pack of cards, learn the attributes and set themselves up in business as a fortune-teller, but they are more than seventy-eight bits of pasteboard in a box. They can be seen as mental triggers, in which by looking at the archetypal images portrayed, the reader's psyche is stimulated and thus enabled to make an interpretation. There are many fanciful theories about their origins, but no one really knows for sure. All that is certain is that the packs appeared in Europe during the Middle Ages and have changed remarkably little in the intervening years.

If you discover that you have an affinity for divination with tarot cards, it is not advisable to charge for the service, not because your work is not worth anything, but because if someone pays you for the service it might encourage you to start 'telling fortunes' instead of performing proper divinations. Of course, this may not bother you, and you may decide you would like to turn card-reading into a career or sideline; if you do, try to keep any financial transactions outside the Pagan circle, because it may cause friction. If you charge for reading the cards of other Pagans, why should a high priestess not be paid for her services? Why should a householder not charge for the use of his or her premises? Before long, Paganism will have become a business; never forget that it is a belief system and not a corporate enterprise.

The cards are not infallible (or, to be precise, you are always likely to make the odd mistake when reading them), but they can be a very valuable aid to concentration when you are faced with a difficult question or situation. In a way, card-reading is a form of meditation like other rituals, because it focuses the mind on to the problem in hand. The best way of learning to use the tarot is to have a look at the packs on offer and pick one that suits you, bearing in mind that most good books are about the traditional 'Rider-Waite' pack, as opposed to the more fanciful recent offerings. Having acquired your pack, take a ring-binder and place seventy-eight sheets of paper inside it, one for each of the cards in the four suits and major arcana or trumps. Then read a few books on the subject and write on the appropriate sheet of paper what they say about the significance of each card. This will depend on the opinion of each author, although there is a solid base of general traditions. Then take your cards one at a time and meditate, letting yourself sink into the pictures and writing down in your folder what *you* feel about each. Never do more than one card a day, and it is better to take your time and get things right than to rush the process and become muddled. You may find that, over the years, your perception of some of the cards changes and grows. When events catch up with the cards' predictions, you may realize that a certain warning was staring you in the face. Learn from the experience and note down which cards you ignored, and what with hindsight you now know they were telling you.

In the initial stages you may find it tempting to consult the cards about anything and everything, such as whether or not to take a bath. Try to avoid such frivolities, not only because they are a waste of time but because the act of reading the cards should be regarded as seriously as any other kind of ritual. Do not demean it by using it to pick lottery numbers or deciding which TV channel to watch, not least because a true tarot reading should be quite a draining experience. It requires a lot of energy, and if you use it indiscriminately, you may find your energies insufficient on those occasions when you genuinely seek the cards' advice.

Another popular method of divination involves the Nordic runes. These are a set of symbols in an ancient alphabet to which meanings have been attached, in much the same way as each tarot card represents a feeling, emotion or state. You can either buy them from a shop or make them yourself by going down to the beach and selecting smooth pebbles, upon which you inscribe the relevant symbols. These are then cast on to a cloth, and can be interpreted from the way they fall and the way the symbols relate to one another.

You might also use the *I Ching*, the Chinese 'Book of Changes'. This ancient text (pronounced 'Yee Jing', and not 'Eye Ching' as most people prefer today) follows a very similar principle to the runes and the tarot. If one casts three coins six times, we have 64 possible heads-and-tails combinations. Each of these corresponds to a chapter in the accompanying book, which contains detailed meditations supposed to inspire an answer in the questioner. This method of divination has been used in China for thousands of years, although originally yarrow stalks were used instead of coins.

The *I Ching*, tarot cards and rune stones are all very similar in their approaches, so if you find one that seems to work better than the others for you, then stick with it and practise until it is second nature. You may find, for example, that the rune stones speak to you in a way that the tarot cards do not. Such differences may depend more on the clarity of the teaching materials than the relevant powers of the methods of divination, or perhaps it is just that the 'click-clack' of the stones helps you concentrate your mind more than the 'flick-flack' of the cards or the 'ching-ching' or the coins. One's preferred method can hinge on such simple, apparently superficial differences.

The Natural World

The skills described above are essentially indoor pursuits. But the real work for a committed Pagan lies outdoors in the world of nature, which is just as much under threat and in need of healing as mankind itself. We have met a lot of folk who claim to be Pagan, but spend most of their lives in their flats or houses, listening to rock music and complaining about the threat to the environment, the iniquities of the government and the immorality of rearing calves in crates. Yet every day is a good day to do a little something to help heal the Earth. At the very least, show your appreciation for the beauty of Nature. Go for a walk through the park and say a silent prayer of thanks for the world around us; perhaps even pick up the odd piece of litter you see lying around. For those of us with relatively easy access to the countryside, there are a number of practical steps that we can take both to enrich our awareness of nature and to actively encourage the healing process. A sense of powerlessness in the face of the problem is not an excuse for inaction.

The most obvious problem is what the individual can actually do. For a start, you can adopt and befriend a tree, something which is possible even in an urban environment. Trees are living creatures just like ourselves, and have spirits that can communicate with us if only we open our minds to their subtle languages. In Greek mythology, there were dryads or wood nymph, who presided as minor deities over the forests, and hamadryads who lived and died as the souls of particular trees. You will have to feel for yourself whether the soul of your particular tree is male, female or androgyne, and certain trees have traditional affinities with certain deities; the willow, for example is sacred to the moon Goddess.

Talking to trees might seem a little odd to some people, but it is only a logical extrapolation of what many do already. Christians talk to God, Pagans talk to the world. Talking to a tree is no stranger than praying to a saint or a god.

You may not have to go looking for a tree. If you wander around and keep an open mind, you may feel a certain tree calling out to you. If you think back to your childhood, did you have a favourite place where you and your friends built a camp or a tree house? Was there a particular glade that felt safer than the others, a good place to sit and read in calm and silence? If you can remember such a place, why not go back there and see if your tree has been waiting there for you?

When you have found your tree, hug it and talk to it about your desires and your worries. It will respond if you can attune yourself properly, and bond by giving out its strength in return for your trust and love. Tell it your secret magical name, and visit it as often as you can. Climb up into it and sit among its boughs to meditate. Bring it gifts, such as a lock of your hair to bury among its roots, and bring an offering of wine to share, as it is an ancient law that what you give in love will be returned to you threefold.

In one of her books, Doreen Valiente describes a very powerful and ancient ritual involving a tree, usually an oak. If your tree is in a lonely place, go there with a partner on a warm summer's night when the moon is full. Undress and dance joyfully around the tree seven times, before lying beneath it and making love in honour of the spirit and fertility of all. When you have finished, take a leaf and moisten it with your sexual fluids, and keep it as a powerful personal talisman.

If there is a well or spring near you, its deity will be an undine or water spirit, and it should be honoured. The ancient custom of well-dressing, which is still practised in many parts of Britain, has Pagan roots, although much of it has now been Christianized. Near Anthony Kemp's home in France there is a *fontaine miraculeuse* which was a place of pilgrimage during the Middle Ages, now sadly neglected. If there is such a place near you, try using the water for ritual purposes; it is likely to be purer than the liquid you get from the taps in your kitchen. You can leave an offering when you visit the well, such as a ribbon tied in the branches of a nearby tree, so that other like-minded folk will know you have been there. You may find that others will leave their offerings, and in time the place will come alive again as its spirit is revived with prayers and human contact. The veil between the worlds is truly thin.

Reactivating the Power of Ancient Sites

Ancient sites exert a powerful attraction on Pagan folk, who feel drawn to places where our tribal ancestors worshipped and lived. Some of these sites are spectacular and well known, such as Stonehenge, Avebury and its associated monuments, Silbury and the West Kennet Long Barrow. In Brittany there is a magnificent alignment of standing stones at Carnac, and the sites in the forest of Broceliande associated with the Arthurian legends. Glastonbury has become a place of pilgrimage and was popular with Pagans long before the recent revival. Although it has been marred by the proliferation of New Age bric-a-brac shops and therapists peddling every conceivable form of psycho-babble, it still remains a place of immense spiritual power. Walking up the Tor at dawn is an emotional voyage into the past which everyone should undertake at least once in their lives. The well-known monuments, however, are generally managed for the benefit of the tourist industry, and have thus inevitably lost much of their attraction for solitary meditators who seek to establish contact with the ancient, group soul of their forebears.

But do not be disheartened. In addition to the great monuments there are thousands of lesser ones scattered all over Europe which have had their powers rendered dormant through neglect, waiting for us to rekindle them. These sites can be discovered from maps and guidebooks in your local library, and they welcome sincere visitors who expect to gain something from communing with their past. They often lie in open countryside far from habitation, in the form of almost flattened burial mounds (marked on Ordnance Survey maps in the UK as tumuli), isolated stones that have fallen over, traces of ancient mazes, settlements and old trading routes. Many medieval churches, now often deserted, were built on Pagan sites, and a little research may be all you need to gain a knowledge of a particular locality and its history. Modern Pagans do not live in the past, but they are aware of the debt they owe to those who went before, and who wove the ancient mysteries that we seek to revive. If you can discover such a site close to where you live, you can perform a simple ritual to make contact with the spirit of the place and, by doing so, reactivate its power as part of the pattern of the land. If that were done at many places, it is likely that the land as a whole could benefit. Large burial mounds, for example, were reserved for a long-forgotten aristocracy and although their location may appear haphazard, the folk who built them must have had a reason for siting them where they did. They would have chosen a propitious place for such a huge endeavour, perhaps on a strong ley line or where they divined a particular source of powerful earth energy. And we can still tune in to that energy.

If you are going to visit such a site, take with you a bottle of wine or some juice to pour as a libation and enjoy as part of a picnic afterwards. When you arrive, sit for a while in meditation and soak in any latent energy, thinking about those who once visited the site or perhaps lived there thousands of years ago. If you feel comfortable and welcome, then you can weave a simple ritual of greeting, which will depend on the nature of the site and whether or not you are alone. But as a basic pattern, you might start by walking clockwise around it, concentrating on the energies of the place and gradually spiralling in towards the centre. When you reach it, kneel down and open yourself, then say the following invocation:

> I/we [*names*] do greet you, spirits of this place and of our tribe from ancient times. Know that you are not forgotten and that we honour your memory. We honour too the great Goddess, the Mother and the great God, her consort. We ask you to awaken from your rest as our Earth is in peril, and give forth again your strength into this land, that it may once again be fertile and blessed. Strengthen me/us that I/we may gain the knowledge to work for what is right in our tribe.

Remain kneeling silently and allow any communications to manifest themselves in your psyche in the form of dreams, visions or sensations. When you feel ready, consecrate the libation and drink to the health of the Old Ones of the place. They too loved a good feast, so unpack your picnic and enjoy yourself alone or with your friends.

When you are ready to depart, bid a fond farewell and thank the spirit of the place. Pour the rest of the libation into the soil and scatter the crumbs of the picnic to share with the wild creatures. If you feel happy with your experience, go back often to talk to the spirit of the place and encourage any like-minded friends to visit them as well. In time, you may build up a small but vital power centre in your locality, and if you leave traces of your visit, others who know the signs will be blessed too if they come upon your sacred place. There are many voyagers in the spirit and flesh, and if you are on holiday elsewhere, seek out the local equivalents of your place, and visit them so that you may see the traces of other, like-minded souls.

Cleansings

There is one other ritual activity which you may have to use at some point, and that is cleansing a dwelling, or ridding it of any bad feelings, the residual energies of others or even the presence of unwanted entities. If you accept the basic premise that every thought and action leaves an imprint somewhere, it follows that the atmosphere of a room or house can become negatively charged if unhappiness was once present. We have all experienced a 'creepy' feeling when entering certain places, but perhaps we do not notice so often the feelings of calm and peace we get when entering others. We do not recommend that you rush out with bell, book and candle and start exorcizing malevolent entities, poltergeists and things that go bump in the night. Such activities are best left to experienced magical practitioners. However, it is quite within your power to cleanse the environment in which you find yourself, and you can do the same for any friends who have feelings of unease in their own surroundings. One such need might, for example, be created as the result of the break-up of a relationship, when you may wish to banish the residual presence of your partner.

The first thing to undertake is a thorough, physical cleansing of the house – not just everyday housework but a truly complete going-over. You must remove all the dust from those hard-to-get-at places you normally ignore – the tops of wardrobes and behind the sofa – anywhere that old dirt may linger. Choose a period when the moon is waning for your ritual, as you will be banishing any unpleasant atmosphere and flooding the space with your love and light. You will need some consecrated water and, if you have one, an old-fashioned broom. The object of the exercise is ritually to make any lingering unease depart and flood the space with light instead, as well as sealing it against any further intrusion. Walk clockwise around your dwelling, symbolically cleansing it as you go and radiating light from within yourself, visualizing yourself and the room as bathed inside and out with bright golden effulgence. This is certainly an occasion for the full ritual bath and the wearing of a clean robe. Anyone else present should also be encouraged to wear something loose and clean if they are not already at home in a Pagan environment.

The following suggestion is based on the cleansing of an apartment with two or more rooms, but it can be adapted to suit any space. In the case of a detached house it is a good idea to perambulate around it on the outside as well if there is a garden; go out and bid the wild creatures of the garden welcome with an offering of seeds and bread. When you are ready, stand with your back to the front door and centre yourself, imagining that you are radiating bright golden light. Then speak an invocation along the lines of the following:

> I call upon the Lady of the moon to bless this place and fill it with her silvery light. O Lady, enter and give peace and comfort to all who dwell here. I call upon the Lord of the sun to bless this place and fill it with his golden brilliance. O Lord, enter in and give your strength and warmth to all who dwell

here. And as the light enters, so shall all that causes sadness and distress be banished, never more to return. So shall it be.

After the invocation, move from room to room clockwise, sprinkling water as you go, chanting around the edges:

Let this place be clean and bright.

At each opening you approach, whether it is a window or door, draw a pentagram with your finger, wand or knife, and imagine it glowing to form a barrier. The pentagram is a very ancient and powerful symbol of protection, which is why so many Pagans choose to wear it. It represents the four basic elements, together with the fifth element which is the spirit, and it is worn with the point upright.

If you are dealing with more than one room, imagine each according to its specific purpose. For example, when you have cleansed and sealed the dining room, filling it with light, imagine the clatter of plates and the laughter and merry conversation of friends or family at dinner. In a bedroom, try to invoke a feeling of peace, love and sleep.

Eventually you will come back to your starting point at the front door. Stand facing it and draw your pentagram, saying the following words or something similar:

So has this place been made clean, and a fitting dwelling for the Lord and Lady of light. Let no one dare to enter with darkness in their mind and may those who dwell here have peace and contentment.

As you do this visualize that you are pushing a dark cloud out of your dwelling and imagine shutting the door firmly with its glowing pentagram aflame. If you have a broom and someone else with you, perhaps the occupant if the dwelling is not actually yours, get him or her to precede you, symbolically sweeping.

Paganism is not an abstract spiritual discipline, although it does contain certain of those aspects for some of its adherents. But above all, it is a living religion in which we can all participate humbly and with joy in our hearts. No one can tell you what you must do; even books such as this can only make suggestions – anything more would be a contradiction of Paganism's deep-seated emphasis on the power of the individual.

But hopefully, the above suggestions may prompt you with some ideas of your own as to how you can contribute to awakening both your own latent faculties and the dormant energies of the land. May your travels be blessed.

9   Further Steps

Paganism is not a religion of easy answers. Having decided to become a Pagan of any sort, the new seeker is inevitably confronted with yet another set of challenges and questions that need answering. Many prefer not to 'come out' but practise their beliefs in solitude, which is perfectly acceptable. Some move from one form of Pagan organization to another as they grow and change. In Wiccan books, especially, you will often read life stories such as: 'X was self-initiated as a Pagan in 1987, and became a first-grade Gardnerian witch in 1992. She is now a priestess of the Order of . . .' This means that the person began in much the same way as the rest of us, with an interest in Paganism that led to personal and private research. She then decided to make a ceremonial pact to affirm her beliefs, in a ritual similar to the self-dedication described elsewhere in Chapter 5. Eventually, as her interest and contacts grew, she ended up joining an established coven, possibly for a couple of years, before splitting off or forming her own group. For all we know, soon after the report was written she may have decided to pursue the solitary Pagan life again, then after a couple more years made a friend at a Pagan gathering and started a little coven of two that soon drew half a dozen more members. This is quite normal.

Many Pagan groups are short-lived, only flourishing for a few years, because we all develop our own idiosyncratic ways of worship and it is often difficult to continue once a certain number of members have left. People may die, move house, emigrate or just get bored. They might leave to set up their own group, or there might be conflicts over personalities or interpretation. These things happen, but it does not matter. Paganism is not like Christianity, where you are told you are joining a club that has been in existence for 2,000 years. Christianity itself has undergone immense changes, schisms and upheavals in its history, but it still claims a supposedly unbroken line. There is a different kind of

Paganism for every Pagan, but covens, hearths, groves and other groups
are not expected to become gigantic edifices with millions of members.
Some covens, of course, do last for a long time, but they are quite rare
phenomena.

The solitary Pagan life has many advantages, including the chance to
experiment and investigate your relationship with the universe on your
own. Much valuable work can be done by a solitary Pagan (a hedgewitch
in Wicca), and it is far better to stay that way than to fall in with a group
who are only Pagans because of the superficial glamour. Other people
may help you understand more about the human race, but there are
times in all our lives when we may need a little space and a little silence.
There is a time for all things, a time to make merry with your friends, a
time to work magic with a group, a time to learn at the feet of a teacher,
and a time to study and meditate by yourself. Our lives are full of such
cycles; there is no more an end to learning than there is to the cycle of
the seasons.

Even if you do set out to pursue a solitary Pagan life, studying and
working in private, there is no guarantee that a prospective coven will
not find you. We dealt with the question of what to tell friends in
Chapter 6. You may find that one or two of your acquaintances show
more than a passing interest and want to get involved themselves, asking
to take part in a ritual or to borrow books. At this stage you often have
to rely on your instincts. Do you want these people to share your spiritual activities? Will they benefit from them or will they think less of you?
Remember the Rede, and ask yourself whether, if you let them take part,
it will 'harm none'. Will it harm your friendship if Paganism is not for
them? Would there be less risk of harm if you lent them a book to read
first, to see if they were still interested? Or if you let them watch a ritual
and then sent them away with a book so that they could comprehend
what was done?

After Anthony Kemp had started out on the path and had some experience working with others, he met his partner and they began to
worship regularly. They soon began to spark an interest in others, and
two women joined what was becoming the nucleus of a coven. As they
made no secret of their beliefs, and generally mixed with 'alternative'
types from the Green Party and similar organizations, their Paganism
was simply accepted. One day in the pub, they were asked what they
were doing for Yule. They replied that they would be celebrating the
festival on the actual solstice, and one or two of the people present asked
if they could come. They thought about the Rede and found the answer

in their hearts: such a request would harm no one, so why not? They ended up with eight of their friends, and the only thing they asked was that everyone should wear something loose rather than street clothing. There was a simple ritual which involved lighting a candle in a darkened room and looking forward to the growing light of spring. Everybody found the experience rewarding and thoroughly enjoyed the party afterwards with mince pies, Yule pudding and wine. That was a one-off occasion, however, as soon afterwards they moved to France, and the small group went their separate ways.

As we have seen, Paganism has until recently kept its light firmly under a bushel, and there are still Pagan groups with very strict rules for admission and initiation. This is not unusual, it is just the way they are run and if you do not like it, you are under no obligation to join. Such groups can be very valuable for providing a structure of learning and a means of meeting like-minded individuals, but they always expect to have trouble with new members, so expect to have to fulfil a few requirements before they let you in. This is only to be expected and should be welcomed as an opportunity to display your commitment.

The most obvious way that such organized groups slow the passage of new members is to insist on several grades of achievement. They may insist that you cannot officially join until a 'year and a day' after you first announce your intentions, on the basis that by then many fair-weather initiates will already have gone on to the next New Age fad, and will not waste their time. Once you are in, they may also insist that you take classes with the senior members and pass different tests of ability, progressing slowly up a hierarchy. This is not necessarily a bad thing, and it does not actually take very long. The groups vary, but in most of them it is possible to get to quite a high rank (for some this might be the third grade, for others the seventh, for still others Elder status) in a few years. Think of it like the process of conversion to Christianity, going through baptism, communion and confirmation. The difference is that 'confirmed' Pagans have the right and ability to lead services themselves. Everyone is a priest, and everyone is the congregation.

The various groups have very good reasons for making your progress through their ranks slower or more difficult than you might want at first, but invariably, amid all the good-hearted seekers of truth there will be the odd person who takes offence at the fact that the order has a sense of order. They may complain, for example, that the grades of a Gardnerian coven imply that some witches are better than others. That is not the case; it is just that those who have been there the longest and

done the most work are liable to have more to teach the others. They
will make similar complaints about the structures of Odinist hearths or
Druid groves. They want *everything, now*, they say inner and outer circles
of knowledge are discriminatory, and that the group is betraying the
principles of Paganism by expecting its members to adhere to rules.

The answer is very simple. If you do not like it, do not go. The choice
is yours. If you respect the group, respect its rules. If you feel that a
certain coven is right for you and it works skyclad, then so must you. If
it has a hierarchy that holds back inner knowledge until you have been
a member for five years and five days, then show your commitment by
staying, or leave. Nobody asks you to join; the decision is yours and
yours alone, and there will be no 'price' to pay if you leave. You will not
go to hell if you leave a group, as is the implication if people turn aside
from a more established religion. You will still be a Pagan, just not one
that feels like belonging to that particular group at that time.

Starting a Group

The Order of Brighid is organized around hearths, each of which is
autonomous and self-governing. A hearth can be a single person, a
couple or a group of friends who share common spiritual aims. This
tends to work well, and we like the symbolism of the hearth as a focus,
with the connotations it brings of warmth and welcoming light. The
person who sets up the hearth is referred to as the Guardian, and he or
she has the right to define its aims and general direction, in consultation
naturally with any other members who are attracted to it. If you find
yourself confronted by others who wish to join you in whatever you are
doing, and you are happy to share with them, forming a hearth is one
way of getting started. There will be nobody breathing down your neck
telling you what to do, and if anyone is not content with the general
policy of a particular hearth, they are at liberty to leave. Moreover, you
do not have to join the Order of Brighid, or anything else for that matter,
to found a hearth.

The best hearths or covens are those that are run on the basis of
mutual consent and shared interests, that regard themselves as clans
which are part of the greater entity of the tribe. Although Paganism is
essentially anarchic in character, any organism however small, requires
some sort of framework. You will need to decide several things before
you start. You should draw up a document together which states your

commitment to the Pagan Rede, and if you are going to worship a specific deity it is a good idea to work out your religious pantheon. There should be some idea of when your group intends to meet, how regularly and with what regard to the passing of the seasons. Will you meet monthly, or more frequently than that? Will you celebrate festivals on the actual days, on the nearest full moon or on the nearest weekend? Is attendance compulsory? If you are hiring a venue, how will you contribute towards the cost? What about refreshments and materials (a big group can get through a lot of candles)? If you intend to meet at each other's homes, you should remember that not everyone will have suitable facilities or open spaces or amenable housemates. Do not force someone to invite eight Pagans round every eight weeks if it will cause trouble. But be fair, and make sure that each member is contributing something of equal weight to your operations.

Who is going to perform the rituals and how will the responsibility rotate, if at all? If you are going to have a hierarchy, who will teach whom, or will that rotate and will you share responsibilities for teaching in different areas? How will someone be examined? Who is responsible for doing what, both within the ceremonies and out in the daily world? There may be other benefits to group membership, which you can work out with your fellows. One hearth we know of has joint membership of a book club, and is establishing a reference library for the benefit of all its members.

You should also have some idea of what you are expected to wear during your meetings. Will you be naked, or will you have some sort of special clothing? Something different is certainly recommended, be it a colour or a type of clothing. Will you have a symbol or sign that will bind you together as a group, such as a pendant or a ring?

You should also make sure that you have come to some kind of arrangement about non-members. Can minors attend? This is both a question of baby-sitting for members with children, and one of new members. If you were approached by a 15-year-old runaway, who wants to 'be a witch', for example you could write the 'DEVIL CULT KIDNAPS TEENAGER' tabloid headlines yourself. There should be an agreement about the presence of minors, both to avoid accusations of corrupting youth, and to prevent misunderstandings about children at meetings. Some groups may be able to provide crèche facilities, some may invite nursing mothers to be active participants in the meetings, others may prefer to have a policy of no children in case they misbehave during a serious ritual.

You may be approached by outsiders, either wishing to join or requesting that you 'cast a spell' on their behalf. There should be a policy on this that is acceptable enough, just to make sure that your newest member does not turn up after a week and announce that she has agreed to use magic to make her brother-in-law win the lottery. If seekers wish to join the group, how fast should they be brought into the circle? A probationary period of a year and a day is heartily recommended. Very few of your initial enquirers will still be around after such a long period, but it is best if they storm off *before* you take them into your confidence rather than to sign them up and find they become bored after three weeks and tell everyone in the neighbourhood misguided tales about what you are doing. You should also work out how such people will be initiated, if at all.

Finally, you should also discuss the breaking up of a group. It may sound pessimistic, but the chances of the same people meeting in the same place, on the same timetable for more than, say, seven years, are quite remote. People will move house, get married, change denominations and fall out, and it is good to have several policies ready before such actions take you by surprise. If an argument starts within the group, how will it be resolved? If someone breaks your rules, how should it be dealt with?

Hopefully, many of these problems can be resolved quite easily if your screening process at initiation is good enough. If the trendy short-timers can be scared away, if the ignorant can be defeated by being sent away to read books, and if misconceptions can be nipped in the bud by the availability of a charter or rule book, the running of your group should be fairly smooth.

It does not hurt, either, to have a secret ballot on new members so that anyone with misgivings can air them without personal attack. Groups generally develop a ritual whereby a new member is brought into the group and swears to support its policies and be loyal to the others. The ritual of self-dedication can be adapted for this purpose, without the nakedness if that is not the custom. If all new initiates were obliged to swear not to reveal anything they learn for a seven-year period, you will know that your operations will not be broadcast from the rooftops if a member leaves. If your group has emergency procedures for banishing uncooperative members as a last resort (including, say, majority votings on a secret ballot), that could stop the group itself being torn asunder by an argument over a particular member.

Finally, you will have to decide on a name for your group – which will almost certainly be harder than you imagine, as you argue about how to spell it – and to prepare for your first ritual. The one listed below is particular to the Order of Brighid, and is offered as an example only. Some people may find it problematic if they do not possess a genuine hearth or fireplace, but a candle or charcoal brazier can serve as a symbol. Others may wish to choose a particular stone as their symbol, especially if there is no actual fireplace available.

Having lit the fire, prepare a plate with small twigs, one for each person who will be present. Ensure that you also have some cooled ash, either in front of the grate or on a dish. You will also need some powdered incense or a bowl of dried and pleasant-smelling leaves or flower petals. A suitable stone should be selected and washed under running water and then consecrated. It should then be placed either by the grate or in front of the charcoal burner, to serve as the hearthstone. The ritual is celebrated by the person who will be the Guardian of the hearth, in the presence of those who will be members. For the sake of convenience the directions below assume a female Guardian, but it could be a man, or a couple could be joint Guardians.

All participants enter duly bathed and robed, and the temple or working space is opened in the manner outlined in Chapter 5. The Guardian then kneels before the fire and in her own words swears an oath of service and invokes her aspirations for her hearth. She then turns to the others who may be present and asks if they will accept membership and be loyal to her as Guardian. Assuming agreement, she then says:

> Beloved brothers and sisters, I do welcome you in perfect love and perfect trust.

She goes to each in turn and greets them with a kiss.

> Draw near with me and help me to feed the sacred flame, that it may nourish and warm all those who will worship in this place.

She takes a twig and places it on the fire, offering a prayer. She then offers the other twigs to the participants in turn, each of whom also offers a prayer:

> As the flames ascend to give us light, let sweet incense burn and give us inspiration.

She casts a pinch of incense on the fire, followed by each in turn of the other participants.

> As we are all agreed to worship and serve together at this hearth, then let us do it honour.

She kneels and kisses the hearthstone, and then marks her forehead with the symbol of the circle cross in ash. Each member then comes forward in turn to kiss the stone and have their foreheads marked with the circle cross by the Guardian. She then says:

> With this solemn rite, I declare the hearth of [*chosen name or deity*] open. May it ever remain a beacon of love, light and warmth, to give a welcome to those who seek the knowledge of the Lady and the Lord, her consort. So shall it be.

This could be followed by each member presenting a gift to the hearth – a book, a candlestick, incense or a pack of candles. Finally, all members should celebrate such a happy occasion by sharing food and wine in the circle together.

Patterns of Worship

Having set up a hearth, either alone or with others, the inevitable question is what to do next? Paganism has no set pattern of worship, but most traditions tend to work around the moon cycle. As far as individual worship is concerned, those who are well organized in their daily lives may decide on a regular daily time for prayer or meditation. Even ten minutes sitting or kneeling quietly can do wonders in healing the stress of everyday life, and it is worth finding the time, as well as being an excellent form of self-discipline.

There is no corpus of rituals laid down in the form of a set pattern of worship; in traditional witchcraft nothing was written down and the transmission of knowledge went from mouth to mouth. Possession of a ritual book was a passport to the gallows or the torture chamber, and many of the wise men or women of the village would in any case probably have been illiterate. Paganism acknowledges from the outset that rituals will differ from group to group, and may even change over time within the same group.

In Wicca, each new witch is required to copy out the coven's *Book of Shadows* by hand, which is itself a very useful discipline. If you decide to use the rituals in this book, for example, you could copy the ceremonies into a book of your own, embellishing or adapting them as you do so until they seem right for you and your own group. You may even wish to decorate your book to show your respect; and we have seen such manuals beautifully embellished with drawings, pressed flowers and all sorts of symbols. If you have terrible handwriting, there is no problem in using a word processor, do not scorn modern technology in favour of a goose quill pen if the end result will be illegible.

Most Pagans who do not follow any particular fixed tradition tend to develop their own methods of worship, and we strongly urge any student to start his or her own book or books, which should be kept in a secure place and not shown to others. Some prefer ringbinders to spellbooks, since that allows the rituals to be shuffled and updated as necessary. Thus, for example, if you write or obtain a new ritual for Samhain, you can simply insert it in the relevant place. Those who start off on the Path generally tend to use published material, but as they gain in confidence they invariably adapt, mix and match and eventually start writing ceremonies that are all their own. If you see a poem or invocation in a book or magazine that moves your emotions, copy it down into one of your folders, together with a note of its source and author. You may even find rituals in the miasma of the Internet. Try typing Pagan, Wicca or Witchcraft into your search engine to get an idea of what covens are up to on the other side of the world.

In addition to a book of rituals, you are strongly advised to keep a magical diary, a strictly personal record of any spiritual activity you may undertake. This should include, besides the time, place and purpose, any psychic experiences, personal comments, your mood or feelings and any results. It is also a good idea to record the exact wording and methods of any magical activity you tried, since you may find that you get what you actually asked for, rather than what you wanted. Such records can be extremely helpful in honing your magical skills, experimenting with new methods and getting better results.

As Paganism is so individualistic in its origins, each of us instinctively knows when is the right time to worship. As a bare minimum, it is generally accepted that the eight festivals are a decent cycle for modern Pagans. Most people celebrate all eight, either alone or in the company of others, using a ritual already published or creating one to suit the occasion that reflects their own membership and beliefs.

Moon Magic

Wiccan covens generally meet at the full moon, and thus a word or two is appropriate about moon magic in terms of a monthly ritual pattern. The new moon is a time for fresh beginnings, celebrating a new endeavour or working magic for the renewal of oneself or a friend. As the moon waxes so its power increases, and that is a time for tuning into that energy for the achievement of positive ends. Magically, that could mean working for someone to pass an examination, for healing, for selling a house, for finding a loving partner and so on. On the night of the full moon, the witches are celebrating everywhere, and it is a good time to emphasize magically any work done at the new moon, since this will boost the strength of the spell.

Then, as the moon wanes, its energy changes and it is the time for banishing, getting rid of bad influences or negative aspects that may be affecting your life or those of others. That is not 'black magic', consciously using the forces of evil, but a positive force to banish anything that hinders the achievement of good. There is nothing wrong in that.

To sum up, the new moon is a suitable time for dedications, initiations, the start of a new job or business venture, or perhaps a fresh start in a new house or flat. As the moon energy grows towards the full, work for anything that requires a positive outcome such as healing, cementing a relationship or success in examinations. Use the waning moon for banishing unpleasant influences, cleansing a new dwelling or preparing for a new start at the new moon.

10 Pagan Parenting

In their book *Eight Sabbats for Witches*, Janet and Stewart Farrar published rituals for child dedication, marriage and death, but these were written in a solely Wiccan context and are only really suitable for working in a coven. However, as more and more people accept Paganism as the spiritual framework for their lives, there is an increasing demand both for suitable rituals for such occasions and for members of a priesthood to perform them. As a worthwhile start, the Pagan Federation now maintains a list of people who are prepared to carry out child blessings, marriages and so on for those who do not have the necessary contacts within their own circle of friends. After all, it is not very easy to do your own wedding, and quite impossible to conduct your own funeral.

Public celebrations to mark the various stages in an individual's life are among the earliest recorded examples of religious practice. We all have a basic need to belong to a tribe or clan, and it is through ceremonies that a sense of belonging is imparted. In the Western world, where the tribal nature of society has largely been destroyed, we have had to invent different ways of signifying our status within society. The football fan proudly wears the regalia of his team, the old soldier his regimental blazer and the Old Etonian his tie. Although Christianity is in decline there is still a massive demand for church weddings, and many couples still firmly believe in having their children baptized, in spite of the fact that they never attend a place of worship. Many is the funeral we have attended in a bleak municipal crematorium where the local vicar has muttered a few platitudes and pocketed his fee without even knowing or caring particularly about the deceased.

The following sections offer some practical suggestions for ways in which Pagans might celebrate rites of passage for both themselves and their families, with or without the assistance of a priestess or priest. As usual, no hard and fast dogma is laid down; these are merely our suggestions, to be used or not as you see fit. As Paganism becomes more widely accepted, such celebrations may well include guests from other faiths – just because we are not Christians, it does not mean that we would refuse to attend the wedding of a friend if invited.

Paganism and Your Children

The subject of child-rearing within Paganism has only recently been given much thought. Modern Paganism is such a young religion that it has only recently had to face several issues which have been long-established in other religions. Pagan parenting is one such area, because Paganism as a way of life has initially appealed mainly to young people. Most Pagans are not born into the tradition, because modern Paganism itself has not been around long enough for many people to have met, married and raised children in the tradition. We are now seeing more and more Pagans by birth, but the phenomenon is relatively recent.

Generally speaking, people adopt Paganism as adults. There is a preponderance of women in the tradition, especially single mothers, but even today there is considerable reluctance to involve children. The solemnity of the rituals can be difficult to maintain with children running around and clamouring for attention, but more importantly Paganism's confusion with Satanism in the eyes of many people has made the issue of child Pagans fraught with peril. Many Pagan parents are paranoid that armies of social workers will descend on their houses the moment they get a whiff of witchery or the flash of a silver pentagram under a small shirt. There are still folk with children who prefer to keep their activities secret, both from outsiders and from their own offspring, in case they suffer persecution or even prosecution. Several years ago in the UK there was a spate of allegations about ritual Satanic abuse, which brought these fears to the fore in the tabloid press, but the collapse of the cases led to a far more open attitude, and even to the appointment of a Parent Liaison Officer by the Pagan Federation, which is to be greatly welcomed. Today there are far more children being brought up in Pagan households, and inevitably parents are asking questions about coping with school authorities.

The whole issue of 'coming out', which can even split Pagan groups which do not have the burden of children, is particularly problematic for parents. Do you attempt not to rock the boat by concealing your religious affiliations, hoping that you will never be 'found out' by ignorant people, yet fearing that they will use your secrecy as another weapon against you? Or do you boldly announce your affiliation, hoping thereby to make it clear that you are proud to be a Pagan, and that it is nothing to be ashamed of, yet secretly hoping that only sensible people, who appreciate what a Pagan is, hear you? The degree to which people 'come out' is their own affair. Everyone is guaranteed the right to practise their religion freely, and politicians never cease telling us how proud they are of our modern, multicultural, multi-faith society. It seems, however, that the degree of acceptance of a religion depends upon the number of its potential voters and the efficacy of its relationship with the media. Race also plays a considerable part: anyone making adverse comments about Islam or Rastafarianism is likely to be branded a racist, but in the Anglo-Saxon world Pagans tend to be white, and are therefore a soft target. In many schools in inner city areas these days, children from a Christian background are in a minority, yet lack of understanding and, at times, blatant discrimination is a frequent theme of letters to Pagan magazines, and Pagans get very annoyed when the tabloid press publishes another 'exposé of child abuse by witches'.

Pagans accept that they do not own their children, but are their guardians until they reach the age at which they can choose their own way of life. Children are little souls; they bear their parents' genes, but in other respects they have to decide for themselves what and where they want to be. During the period of guardianship, however, the parents have the responsibility for bringing up the children in such a way as to encourage them to make sensible choices when the time comes, and to give them a strong moral background. We do not believe that we can force our religion down the throats of our children, any more than we have the right to proselytize non-Pagans. Having said that, it is perfectly reasonable to give them the experience of sharing in our spiritual activities; we should just not pressurize them into committing themselves. The Pagan religion is full of ex-Catholics who have revolted against the religion that was forced upon them in their youth. This chapter contains a ritual for blessing and naming a child, but that does not make it a Pagan; it simply invokes the protection of the deities until the child is old enough to choose its own spiritual path.

The extent to which Pagan parents should involve their children in their religion is obviously a matter of individual choice, influenced by the nature of their denomination, since children are easier to integrate if ceremonies involve a quick prayer and a feast, rather than a complex magical working requiring silence, meditation and concentration. For legal reasons, many Wiccan covens will not permit minors to join, and the year and a day that many Wiccan novices are expected to wait is particularly useful for gently turning away immature applicants; 366 days is a long time if you are fourteen.

There are also high magical rituals that could easily be ruined by children, and others that are not permitted to be seen by non-initiates, which would of course exclude children from the outset. However, the various religious festivals of the year are eminently suitable for the participation of younger members of the congregation. Take a leaf from the Catholics' book. In principle at least, they involve children in the enjoyable ceremonies from an early age, but do not ask them to confirm their religious affiliation and join the more complex catechisms until they are in their mid-teens.

It may also be that your children are simply not interested in your religion, and as a parent you should respect their views. But if they show a modicum of interest, it is right and proper that you should answer their questions, rather than leave them to guess at what is going on. The age at which such questions might occur will vary according to the child's inquisitiveness and the degree of religious stimulus he or she receives in the home. Some parents prefer to reserve any religious activity for the time after the children have gone to bed, but once they are older, why not allow them to participate in suitable rituals, if they ask? Yule is often a good time to start. The child will usually be thinking about Christmas anyway, and you can explain that the festival is the time when the Pagans also celebrate and give each other presents. If you then find that your child is seriously interested, working through the festivals will teach him or her about the pattern of the seasons, the beauty of the God and Goddess legends, the sacredness of food and the nature of death and rebirth.

One note of warning however. While you may think your children are ready to join your group, there may be members of the group who do not agree. If all the coven or hearth members have children, there is less likely to be a problem, but do not expect non-parents to share your interest in your children. If other members of your group prefer children to be left out of the rituals, you should respect their wishes, either by separating family and coven or hearth life, or suggesting a splinter group of parents, so as not to disturb those who find children distracting. Do as you will, but harm none, and some people just do not like children, especially in a religious setting.

The jointly chosen chief of the British Druid Order conducting a public hand-fasting rite at Avebury stone circle. All walks of life are represented in the Pagan community

Clonegal Castle in Ireland, the site of the foundation of the Fellowship of Isis

One of the many beautiful altars in the shrine at Clonegal Castle. Note the incorporation of Egyptian symbolism

A more simple altar decoration prepared for a Pagan ceremony

Meditation is the key to progress along every spiritual path. The choice of position and surroundings is up to the individual

The moment of consecration. In the Wiccan rite the sword represents the male and as it is lowered into the chalice (female) the mystery of the creation of life is symbolically enacted

Anthony Kemp conducting the blessing and naming of Alexander Christopher in his garden temple in France

A Pagan preparing to consecrate the wine for a ceremony in her temple

Doreen Valiente standing in front of an old tree stump called 'The Naked Man' which marks the old witches' meeting place in the New Forest

The Naming and Dedication of a Child

The birth of a child is a joyous occasion and a just cause for celebration. As we have said, Pagans do not believe in imposing their beliefs on their children, and most accept that any ritual marking new arrivals is more for the benefit of the adults than the children. The children will have their chance to decide later in life; they are not Pagans purely because they have had a Pagan naming ceremony. The purpose is not for the community to gather in new souls, but rather to invoke the protection of the God and Goddess until such time as the children are old enough to choose their own path. J.M. Sertori was asked to celebrate a ritual for a little boy aged six who, of his own accord, wanted to feel part of his mother's religion, as he had not been 'done' at birth. Not all Pagans feel the need for such ceremonies, and there is no obligation, but many parents feel that it is right to have some sort of ceremony even if it is purely to welcome their child into the wider community.

Individual traditions have their own customs. Wiccans call the ceremony of dedicating a child 'Wiccaning', and it is normally carried out within the confines of the parents' coven, although it can also be celebrated by the high priest and high priestess in the presence of friends. A fairly common ritual is the one written by the Farrars, in which the high priest presides in the case of a female child, and his high priestess for a male. This, they feel, creates the essential polarity. They also introduce the possibility of sponsors or godparents, who do not necessarily have to be Pagans, as long as they are in sympathy with the basic principles involved in the ritual. It is obviously good for a child to have the support and friendship of other adults, but there are those who find the notion of godparents too Christian, and sponsors too sterile. Personally, we prefer the notion of a godfather or goddess-mother if suitable people are available, but again it is a matter of individual choice.

There is no reason whatsoever why the parents should not name and dedicate their child without any outside assistance. The best way is to take the baby to a sacred site or place where there is a natural spring, say a prayer to the gods for their blessing and protection, sprinkle the child with water and call out his or her name to the deities. In the days before the Stonehenge Free Festival was banned by the authorities, it became a tradition for children to be named within the stone circle after sunrise at the summer solstice. Rainbow Jo, a poetess and priestess, took her daughter to Chalice Well in Glastonbury to name her, and wrote:

I am an animal earthed with her birth
She is the wild rose of this summer's blooming
Clear as a crystal, a gift held in trust
She is the wise one, the wild one, the old one
Earth-child, Moon child and daughter of witches
All that is manifest, held in a moment.

Much depends on the season of the year, however. The northern European climate is hardly conducive to stripping a young child naked in the woods in winter and pouring cold water on to him or her. The ritual can therefore be performed indoors in the warm, using pure bottled mineral water which can be consecrated beforehand if required. If the parents feel unable to perform the ceremony themselves or do not wish to do so, they can ask a Pagan friend or member of the priesthood to do it for them. It is a great honour for a priest to be invited to dedicate and bless a child, as he or she is a new little star.

The following is Anthony Kemp's personal ritual for such occasions, which can be adapted to suit the needs of those concerned. It can be done simply and quickly or celebrated with great ceremony; in a woodland glade, on a beach or in a magnificent temple; the participants can be dressed in ordinary clothes or asked to wear robes. If there are non-Pagans present, the rite should be explained to them beforehand, and afterwards there should be a bit of a party, as birth is a time of great joy. Also, gifts should be given to the child – a silver amulet perhaps, or a bracelet. The child should be brought to the ritual wrapped in a white robe, towel or shawl, naked underneath. The minimum requirements are for some pure water in a jug, anointing oil and a fresh white candle. If there is to be a more formal ritual, there should be some wine and food to be blessed afterwards.

The participants should gather round the altar with the parents and the child in the centre. The celebrant then consecrates the sacred space according to custom, if it is considered necessary, after which she or he makes an invocation for the deities to be present at the rite. Again, if it is considered appropriate, a brief speech about the purposes of the rite could be made, especially if non-Pagans are present.

The celebrant then asks the parent/s to carry the child forward and unwrap him or her; an older child can be led by the hand. The celebrant takes the water container and sprinkles or pours water over the child, saying:

In the name of the great Goddess, Mother of us all, may this water of life purify and consecrate this her child. What names are given unto her?

The parents give the child's names, and the celebrant says:

So shalt thou be known to those who love you and the sun, the moon and the stars. May their light shine always upon your path so that you will see all that is wondrous within Nature. You are a true child of the Goddess and God of all creation who have fulfilled their promise in the miracle of your birth. In you dwells the essence of the deities in the spark of life itself.

Then the anointing is performed:

I anoint the head of [name] that his/her mind may always seek the truth.
I anoint the hands of [name], that all whom she/he may touch shall be blessed.
I anoint the feet of [name] that the path she/he walks will be in the knowledge of what is right.
I anoint the heart of [name], that it may beat strongly and in love.

O gracious Lady Mother who brings us forth into this world and is with us when we must leave it, only to be reborn, bless this child who has returned to be with us. May she/he grow to know and love you. O mighty Forest Lord, King of all creatures in wood and field, give your strength and blessing to this child. Protect and guard him/her through the difficult journey that lies ahead. I bless and consecrate you, [name], child of the sun and moon. May the guardian spirits be with you until you are old enough to choose your own true path to follow.

The parent/s then swear the following oath, repeating the words after the celebrant:

I/we solemnly swear to love and cherish [name], to protect and care for him/her who has been given to me/us by the

gods. We will teach him/her rightness, truth and love of
Nature, until she/he is of age to follow his/her own chosen
path.

The celebrant then asks if there are any godparents or sponsors. If so,
they are asked to take the following oath:

I/we, in this sacred space and before our gods, do swear to be
a friend to [*name*], and to care for, love and cherish him/her
until she/he be of age to choose the path that she/he will
follow.

The celebrant then lights the white candle and turns to face the parent/s.

Every man and every woman is a star. The flame of this candle
symbolizes the new star who is in our thoughts today. I ask
you all for a moment of silent thought or prayer for [*name*], for
love, light, warmth and merriment in his/her life. I ask too for
your love and support for his/her parents, that they may bring
love, wisdom and understanding to the great responsibilities
and difficult task they face.

At this stage, the mother should wrap the child in a white garment or
shawl or dress it in a white robe. After the few moments of silence, the
celebrant blesses the child, the parent/s and the godparent/s. Then hugs
are exchanged and gifts are presented to the child. If there is to be a
formal blessing of wine and food, this is then done and the meal shared.

You will notice that there is a reference to a child who is old enough
to stand. This could apply when parents who are new to the Pagan
community, and already have a child who is a toddler, ask for a dedication to be performed. There is no real age limit in fact, but with older
children, where nakedness is considered inappropriate, they should
wear a pair of white pants under their robes.

Finally, a word about names. Pagans often like to choose outlandish
names for their children, reflecting their personal preferences. That is as it
should be, and many Pagan names are extremely beautiful, but those who
think them up should also consider what their children will have to face
among their sometimes cruel peers at school. Small Ishtaroths and
Bombadils may grow up to curse their fond parents and long for a more
'normal' handle. A name like Rosehip Rainbird Mugwort Smith could prove

to be something of a disadvantage in the playground. In some Pagan traditions, a child is given a hidden or secret name when it is dedicated, or can either adopt it as a craft name or discard it when he or she grows older.

The Admission of a Child to a Hearth

Children like ceremonies, they enjoy dressing up and the accompanying sense of special occasion. If you encourage your children to join in your celebrations, they should have their own robes which, they should learn, are only to be worn in the temple, and otherwise put away carefully. An inexpensive robe for a child of any age is a plain, white, long T-shirt, tied round the waist with a cord. The same sense of specialness must also apply to any item of ritual jewellery such as an acorn necklace for a boy, or silver bracelets for a girl, which they have to learn to put away after the ceremony and not boast about to their friends. The pre-ritual bath should also be an enjoyable occasion, even for those children who are notoriously water-shy.

When your children reach an age at which they are able to keep quiet, and if they clearly enjoy participating in rituals, you can consider a special act of dedication. This will give them a sense of belonging either to your hearth or to the wider community, without committing them to being Pagans. One Pagan girl, for example, wanted a ceremony of her own after she had seen one of her friends, a Catholic, dressed all in white for her first communion.

The ritual which follows is based on a number of assumptions, but can obviously be adapted to suit different circumstances. It assumes, for example, that the child has both parents, and that they have a hearth, which may include other adult friends and even older children who have already been admitted. But, whatever the circumstances, the most important thing is that the child must *want* to take part, and must have been carefully prepared for what will take place, rather than being pushed into it to satisfy his or her parents.

The child should be given a ritual bath, a boy by his father and a girl by her mother perhaps, and then be dressed in a white robe with a chaplet of flowers on the head. Girls will probably be quite happy, with a long robe but boys might prefer a short one which can be belted around the waist like a Roman tunic, with their legs bare. Underwear should also be white to symbolize the importance of ritual purity and cleanliness in the temple. In the case of a single-parent family, the child can choose a special adult friend or perhaps a godparent to help in the preparation. If the child has a white candle preserved from the naming, it should be carried, lit, into the temple; if not, he or she should be given a fresh one. It should be in a suitable holder, which can be decorated with ribbons or some flowers. While the child is being bathed, any other people present should gather in the temple space and perform the opening ceremony. The child should then be brought in by the person who has bathed and robed him or her, holding the lit candle, and stand at the edge of the circle, facing the celebrant. In the case of a boy who has been bathed by his father, for example, this might be the mother.

The celebrant should ask:

> Have you, [name], come to this temple of your own free will, and do you wish to become a member of the hearth?

If the answer is yes, the celebrant should then take the child's candle and place it on the altar, saying:

> A new bright light has entered into our temple today, and we bid a heartfelt welcome to this child of the Lord and Lady.

The celebrant should then kiss the child and lead him or her by the hand to the centre of the space, where he or she should be asked to kneel or sit. What is then said will depend on the age of the child, but it should be a simple statement about the hearth, the commitment to love and trust between its members, the strength of friendship and the duty to respect all Nature. The celebrant should then take the hearth stone and give it to the child, saying:

> This stone is the symbol of our hearth. Take it and hold it. Feel the strength within it and greet it with a kiss.

When the child has kissed the stone it should be replaced and the child asked to stand. The celebrant should then perform the ritual of purification with the four elements, sprinkling the child with water and salt and passing the incense and candle over him or her. Then the celebrant should say:

> By water and earth, air and fire, are you made pure. Will you promise now to respect the members of this hearth, who in

return will respect you, to treat all things used here with reverence and care and to love the God and Goddess and all the
things and creatures they have created?

Assuming the answer is yes again, the celebrant should than take the oil
and anoint the child on the forehead, saying:

This I anoint you with the sacred oil, and make you a member
of our hearth, blessed child of the God and Goddess. May you
find peace with this space, love, warmth, nurture and understanding always.

The child should kneel again and the celebrant should speak the following prayer, at the end of which he or she will bless the child.

Great Goddess, Mother of all living things and the god, Lord
of the forests and fields, we thank you for the blessed life of
this child [name], and the light it has brought into our lives.
May we who are gathered in this sacred place be given the
understanding and wisdom so to care for and cherish him/her,
that she/he will learn of the beauty of your creation and in due
time be guided on to his/her own true path. While [name] is
in our care, may she/he find love and fulfilment, warmth,
laughter, joy and reverence, and the strength to know about
what is right. This we do entreat and pledge ourselves to
befriend and support our new brother/sister in both times of
joy and sadness. Blessed be, sweet child of the Lord and Lady.

After the blessing, the child should be hugged and kissed by everyone present, who should tell him or her their magical names if they have
them, and offer a gift, which does not have to be expensive, but should
be something to keep, such as a book of legends or about Nature, or
jewellery. The parents could give a pentagram or other amulet to be
worn around the neck if the child does not already have one. Then
everyone should join hands and dance clockwise, chanting or singing
something that the child knows in celebration, like 'The Earth is our
Mother, we will take care of her'. When the dance is finished, all should
sit quietly for a moment before the chalice, which in the case of a child
should be filled with fruit juice or milk, is consecrated. A plate of the
child's favourite biscuits would also be appropriate.

The ritual can end with a party or a special meal at which the child sits in the place of honour. If the child was given a magical name at birth, then it should be used in the temple, but if not, and one is needed, it can be taken at this stage; the child should have the right to choose the name.

The Pagan Child

Once he or she is part of a worshipping community, a child should gradually be given responsibility, such as cleaning brass ritual items, arranging flowers on the altar, lighting the candles or even taking on the role of temple server by passing things to the celebrant during the ritual. Children can also be encouraged to maintain their own private shrines in their bedrooms, decorated with things they have found such as acorns, feathers and interesting shells. The degree of any teaching that may be given depends on the aptitudes and interests of the parents and the extent to which they regard themselves as being part of a religious community following a seasonal pattern of worship.

For many parents, problems occur when a child enters the school system. Do they declare little Ceridwen Moonbeam as a Pagan on the obligatory form under religion, and should they formally withdraw her from assemblies and Religious Education classes? What about the pentagram she wears around her neck? Will that cause trouble when ignorant teachers mistake it for a Satanic symbol?

The best thing to do is to remember the way in which Pagan attitudes differ from those in the world at large. The correct entry on the form is 'brought up in a Pagan household', because children's religious affiliations are their own choice, not that of the people who fill in forms on their behalf when they are still minors. Similarly, there is no reason why you should not allow your child to participate in the assemblies and religion classes of the dominant ideology. Pagans are open to new ideas and new angles on age-old questions, so there is no harm in sending your children along to participate. Perhaps they will learn something, perhaps they will teach the rest of the class something about Paganism.

So much depends upon the viewpoint of the school. If the head teacher or a classroom teacher is militantly Christian, then there is likely to be strife where an overtly Pagan child is involved. That is more likely to occur in areas where there are few people of other religions to stand up for their rights, and thus a lack of experience in dealing with children of other faiths. Everyone has the right of freedom of religious expression, however, and it is really up to the individual parents to decide to what extent they want to exercise that right, bearing in mind that over-strident parents can actually make life harder for their children at school. If in doubt, contact the Pagan Federation for advice.

Another thorny problem is the question of having friends round to the house. Pagans tend to be great collectors of bric-a-brac of an esoteric nature, and some items may well excite the curiosity of small and inquisitive guests. Why has your mummy got a broomstick in the corner? Is she a witch? Why is there a statue of a naked lady on the mantelpiece? These are the sorts of questions that may be asked. There are two ways of handling such difficulties. The first is to exclude children from rooms where such items may be displayed, and the second is to answer such questions openly and honestly. Honesty may be the best policy, but there is a danger that your children may suffer by being ostracized because they are seen as odd. On the whole, children are quite open-minded, but their parents may well be less so. If they come round to collect their offspring from your house and find a huge pentagram on the door, and they happen to be Christians of a bigoted nature, they may rapidly terminate the friendship between your children and theirs. The result may be that your children come to resent your beliefs, feeling they are losing friends because of them.

Unfortunately there are no good manuals for Pagan parents, who simply have to bring up their children as they see fit. One very good organization in which children receive a valuable experience of outdoor life and Nature is the Woodcraft Folk, which was founded just after the First World War as a non-jingoistic alternative to the Scout movement. The Woodcraft Folk are not Pagan, but nor are they overtly Christian. They are closely linked with the Co-operative Movement and tend to become involved with environmental campaign issues. There are also various groups which offer summer camps, for unaccompanied children or for the whole family, which are inexpensive and fun. It may well be that as the number of children in Pagan households increases, more will be done in the way of providing facilities for them to meet others with similar backgrounds and interests. But in the meantime, if you have other Pagan friends, why not organize litter-picking outings to local beauty spots or the beach. This is a worthwhile activity in which children can get involved, and if they just grow up in such a way as not to spray graffiti, wrench wing-mirrors from parked cars or drop litter, the world in which we live cannot fail to be a better place.

Rites at Puberty (Boys)

Generally speaking, those who have made the decision to follow the Pagan way have tended to be relatively young, either unattached or with quite small children. Those who were already on the Path and had older children were of the generation that preferred, or thought it prudent, to exclude youngsters from participating in Pagan customs. Recently, however, the subject of a rite of passage at puberty has cropped up several times in conversations and correspondence, which proves that Pagan folk around the world are thinking along similar lines. The reason is, quite simply, that an increasing number of children are growing up in Pagan households and going through the early life-rituals given above. Now, their families are considering the idea of a form of 'confirmation rite'.

In all religions there are rituals to mark the transition from childhood to adulthood, which for boys often involves undergoing some ordeal, branding or circumcision. Such rites are initiatory in character and confer status within the 'tribe'. In Roman society, boys exchanged their short tunics for the full toga of a man, and in a similar (but less institutionalized) way in our culture, small boys sometimes find the transition marked by the bestowal of their first pair of long trousers. For Jewish children there are the rites of the Bar and Bat Mitzvah, and in Christianity there is the rite of confirmation, in which children reiterate the promises made on their behalf at baptism.

A puberty rite in Paganism presupposes that the child is mature enough to make a decision of some sort. It should never be imposed by the parents for social reasons, as is often the case in Christianity. One of the authors recalls his Catholic father entreating him to agree to confirmation, in fact to swear a binding oath before the Creator of the Universe, not because he believed but because it would placate his grandmother. In many established religions, confirmation is fixed at a certain time in a child's life, hence the pressure on Catholics of a certain age to be confirmed, and for Jewish boys to have their Bar Mitzvah at the same time as their peers. But children differ immensely in their spiritual development, and while some may be ready to join the community as fully fledged worshippers at twelve or thirteen, others may prefer to wait until they are older, or may simply remain indifferent. The decision on whether to perform such a rite should remain a matter between children and their parents, and must never be forced upon anyone as a matter of form. Children will know if they feel ready to take such a step.

Rites at puberty are initiatory in character, but they are not initiations as the term is understood within some sections of the Pagan community, which is only offered to mature adults. The following is an outline for a ceremony for a boy. In keeping with the old ways he should submit himself to an ordeal of some description to signify the acceptance of adult responsibilities and the sacrifices involved. Ideally, the father should be involved, together with any other close male adult friends the boy may have and trust – a godfather perhaps or members of his father's clan. In the case of a boy who has grown up with his mother, she may, with her son's agreement, choose a suitable adult male friend for the ritual. The ordeal could involve making a shelter in a wild place and sleeping out alone for a night, undertaking a trek or climbing a mountain with a group of men. Ideally, it should involve physical effort and be out of doors, perhaps using tools, as in cutting wood for a fire or making a shelter. If an outdoor activity is inappropriate, the boy should spend some time alone as a form of vigil, in a room sparsely furnished without distractions such as computer games, television or toys.

Once the ordeal or vigil is completed, men should prepare a suitable place, either in the woods or in a temple room. They will need water, salt, a candle and incense on the altar, anointing oil, a loose robe and cord for the boy and some (removable) body paints. If the ceremony is to be conducted outdoors, a fire is essential and some spring water if available. A good idea would be to have a drum or drums and a gift such as a knife to symbolize the taking on of responsibility. And if the ritual is to have any real impact on the boy it must be a truly mystical experience which will depend very much on the attunement and sincerity of the participants.

When the ordeal has been completed, the boy should be bathed by his father – in a stream, lake, river or just the bath, and then dressed simply with a piece of cloth wrapped around his waist and a pair of shorts or pants; he should be naked above the waist. He should then be blindfolded and his hands tied behind his back, and he should be brought to the place where the ritual is to be performed. If it is outdoors, he will feel the earth under his naked feet, sense the warmth of an open fire and hear a gentle drumbeat. At the threshold, he will be asked if he is willing to take on the responsibilities of adulthood and to enter into the company of the men of his clan. Having affirmed this, his father and the other men should paint him with the symbols of the hearth, either on his forehead or on his whole upper body, in spirals or other designs. He will feel the fingertips brushing his skin.

The next stage is the confrontation with the elements, starting in the east. The boy is led to that quarter, and will hear the voice of his father or another man speaking something along the lines of the following (if the ceremony is indoors, the incense should be passed over the boy's body):

Behold thou art in the east and in the realm of air. Feel the gentle breeze upon thy body, and breathe in the blessed winds. Fill thy lungs with the sweet scents of nature and be purified. I call upon the elemental guardians, the Lords and Ladies of the winds, to guard and protect this boy, [name], as he becomes a man.

The boy should then be led to the fire and positioned close enough so that he can feel the heat on his skin but not suffer discomfort.

Behold thou art in the south and in the realm of fire. Feel the heat upon thy body and fear it not. Fire can burn but it also cleanses. So shall it make thee pure. I call upon the elemental guardians, the Lords and Ladies who tend the sacred fires, to guard and protect this boy, [name], as he becomes a man.

He is then taken to the west where he should be sprinkled with some water and given some to drink.

Behold, thou art in the west, the realm of the healing waters. Feel the waters of life and intuition on thy skin and drink deeply from the cup. Thus shalt thou be purified. I call upon the Lords and Ladies, the guardian of the sweet springs and wells, to guard and protect this boy, [name], as he becomes a man.

Lastly, the boy is led to the north of the space and presented to the earth guardians, where he should be sprinkled with salt or soil.

Behold thou art in the north, in the realm of earth, where dwelleth our Lady Mother and her consort, the Lord of the forests and of all the beasts and men. As the earth was given to us, so must we care for it and I solemnly charge you in this sacred space that that must be your task. Great Mother and

mighty Lord, and all the Lords and Ladies of the Earth, I call
upon you to guide and protect this boy, [name], as he
becomes a man.

By this stage all the boy's senses should be heightened and the drumbeat should speed up a little as he stands, sensing the presence of others.
He should then be given a token infliction of pain – a brief slap across
the cheek or a stroke with a thin stick. The essential element is a short
shock, administered with the words:

Know you well, boy, that the way ahead to manhood will
bring much pain as well as pleasure, grief and sadness, light-
ness and darkness. We are taught that to learn we must first
know suffering. And now, thou shalt be given thy freedom.

The hands should be untied and then the blindfold removed.

Walk proudly as a man but in humility before the gods and
goddesses. Let your eyes see the beauty of Nature and of
others, regardless of their race or origin, rich and poor alike.
As you give love, so shall you receive it.

The father or other person should take the oil and anoint the boy on
the forehead, the palms of his hands, the soles of his feet and his heart,
making similar invocations as those used in the child dedication ritual.
He should then be asked to approach the altar and make his dedication
or vow in his own words, after which he should be clothed and the cord
tied around his waist.

That ends the ritual itself, as he is then welcomed and given a hug by
all present. A speech can be made and he can be presented with a knife or
other suitable gift, and offered a token drink from a consecrated cup. A
further refinement would be for a lock of the boy's hair to be ritually burnt,
or for him to offer up a symbolic sacrifice to the fire of something he trea-
sured in childhood – a stuffed animal, a toy or an article of clothing.

Rites at Puberty (Girls)

The rite for girls can be similar in general structure, with a few basic
changes. The men should not be involved, just as the women are

excluded from the boys' ritual. The most obvious difference is in the ordeal, which does not need to be specially arranged. The girl's ordeal is internal, her first period, and it is the onset of menstruation that symbolizes her entry into womanhood. Thus a girl's ritual is not about her own decision to become an adult, but about the fact that she already is!

The ritual of elemental dedication is the same, but in the case of a girl, it should be preceded by a discussion. This can take any form; some are wild parties like the classical bacchanals, others might be a simple chat in a circle. Whatever the format, this is the chance for the other members of the clan to discuss their feelings and experiences. The boy's ritual emphasizes trial and ordeal, becoming a man by showing strength and bravery. The girl's emphasizes acceptance and inner power, becoming a woman by showing a different kind of strength. Girls do not expel their demons by putting themselves through a tough experience, instead they must 'talk out' their problems. Girls' puberty rituals are a chance for all the women to discuss their pasts and their experiences, to support each other by demonstrating that they are not alone in the world, and to carry each other through the trials and tribulations that they will all face. Just as the male ritual conceals within it a symbolic announcement of brotherhood and support, by talking through their experiences the female ritual symbolically informs the new arrival that she is part of a group, that she will always have their support, and that the secrets they share within the circle will bind them together in the outside world. Both ultimately say the same thing: that you are not alone, that you will never be alone while you are a Pagan, because you have joined a society that aspires to perfect love and perfect trust. Paganism brings you friends in the spirit world, but also friends in the everyday world.

11   Handfastings and Farewells

Marriage

Even in this materialistic age, the issue of marriage has ancient tribal customs and taboos bubbling very close to the surface: the ordeal of the sheer expense (if it costs money, it might remind us how solemn are the vows we are making), the dressing-up, the coming together of the members of two different tribes – even a Christian wedding comes loaded with Pagan symbolism. Although in Western society virginity is no longer a prized commodity which has to be proved on the wedding night, many brides will still wear the white dress and veil which symbolize purity. What Pagan can fail to chuckle at a Christian groom's ritual overindulgence to purge himself of wanderlust, a final sowing of wild oats called, of all things, a 'stag night', and the equivalent women's ritual, with the sexes split to indulge in their own secret mysteries on the night before the wedding? Paganism and its role in our ancestors' lives is made very clear at a wedding, as is the role of ritual and symbol in our lives. The religious significance is not important – the rituals are basically the same in every religion from Shinto to Judaism. What is important is how those rituals remind the participants of their roles and duties in life. This is what Paganism seeks to do in every area of our lives, not merely the so-called 'best day' (which implies it will be downhill all the way, from then on!), in which we swear undying love.

Wicca adopted the old gypsy word 'handfasting' for its marriage rite, and the one used in the Farrars' book was adopted from the novel *Sea Priestess* by Dion Fortune. Others have devised suitable rituals for their friends, but once again, there is no format set in stone. In some Wiccan groups, there is the notion that a couple can be handfasted for a year and a day, so that a marriage requires continual renewal of the vows every

366 days. Although this may serve to keep both participants on their toes, it can also backfire. Part of the significance of marriage lies in the acceptance of a long-term commitment. The Christian marriage is quite specific on the matter of 'for better for worse, for richer for poorer', and the bride and groom are expected to help each other through difficult times. The 366-day Wiccan handfasting is thus not recommended as a serious marriage ritual, although as a ritual of betrothal or engagement (a 'dry run' for a more long-term commitment), it is heartily recommended.

Pagan weddings have been celebrated in woodland glades with just a couple of friends present, or in hired halls with considerable ceremony before an assembled throng. It really depends on the tastes of the participants and to what extent they wish to have their exchange of vows witnessed by friends and family – some members of the family may be willing participants in a Pagan ceremony, others may refuse to attend on principle.

At the most basic level, the loving couple should go to a chosen spot which is special to them, and make their commitment to each other alone or in the presence of the gods. One of the most delightful Pagan marriages we have encountered took place at the ancient maze on top of St Catherine's Hill outside Winchester. The couple invited their friends to join them by walking the maze, and when everyone reached the centre they all joined hands to make a circle. Thus surrounded by family and friends at a sacred, ancient place, the bride and groom exchanged their promises and rings.

Recent changes in British law make it possible for a registrar to attend religious ceremonies at suitable places, which can be private rooms in hotels or halls, and witness the signing of the register. That considerably simplifies the legal side of a religious ceremony, but sadly does not cater for those who wish to marry beside a waterfall in a remote corner of Wales, or in a hot air balloon.

The following ritual is offered purely as an example, and it can be adapted as needed. It is the intention that counts, not the form of words used, as Pagans do not accept the ritual as social convention. Yes, there is often a great deal of partying afterwards and the participants should wear their best robes, but the commitment they make is to each other in the presence of the gods, and not just something to please their grandmothers. The celebrant can be a close friend, a friendly witch or a priest or priestess.

This ritual assumes that at the very least the couple and the person who will perform the ceremony, either indoors or outdoors, are present. All that is required is some anointing oil, two lengths of red cord to bind the couple's wrists and ankles, a white candle and the rings or other tokens that they will exchange. Before the ceremony they should write down in their own words the form of the vows they wish to exchange with each other, as these cannot be imposed by anyone else. The celebrant only channels the energy, without representing an authority or 'church', but he or she can give advice. The trappings of the ceremony will depend upon the circumstances and most couples will wish to invite their friends to celebrate with them, as well as to wear special clothes. Both bride and groom can select a special friend to attend them, and children to act as bridesmaids or pages. A wedding is a wonderful occasion for dressing up, and if the bride and groom already have children, this is the perfect way to involve them in their parents' new situation.

If the ritual is conducted indoors, the temple can be decorated with flowers and lit by masses of candles, and the altar placed in the east. If there are guests, especially people who are not used to Pagan ways and may feel awkward, someone should be appointed as usher to show them where to sit (in the west) and it is a good idea to have printed sheets with the wording of the ritual. When everyone is ready, a chosen person goes to fetch the bridegroom and his attendant and place him in the south, where the celebrant greets him with a kiss. Then the bride and her attendant or attendants are brought forward and she is placed in the north with another kiss of welcome. The celebrant speaks the following words:

> Blessed friends, we have gathered together in this sacred place to celebrate the marriage between this woman, [name], and this man, [name]. Such a marriage transcends any purely legal commitment made before a representative of the state, because it is celebrated before the deities and thus cannot be entered into lightly or set aside with impunity. Since ancient times, marriage has been a custom wherein a man and a woman are joined together for mutual support, love and care, and if so destined, their union can be blessed and enriched with children.

The celebrant then turns to the man and addresses him:

> O man, behold thy chosen woman and gaze upon her beauty. Thou must know that she is made in the image of the

Goddess, glorious and beautiful, strong and wise, priestess
and mother. See in her thy fulfilment in love and companion-
ship. See in her thy inner feminine self and rejoice that in her
thou mayest find fulfilment. See in her womanhood the grail
of immortality, the sacred cauldron that is the very cradle of
life itself.

Then the celebrant turns to the woman.

O woman, behold thy chosen man and gaze upon his beauty.
Thou must know that he is made in the image of the God,
strong and upright, the protector of the weak, who shall be thy
loyal soulmate. See in his manhood the sword of power from
which flows the very force that gives us life. Rejoice in the
strength of his embrace and be whole.

The bride and groom are then led to the centre of the circle and made
to face each other. The celebrant takes the anointing oil and hands it to
the man, who anoints his lady on the forehead, saying some suitable
words of honour. The bride then anoints her man in a similar fashion.
The celebrant says:

Duly made sacred with the consecrated oil, your bodies shall
be worthy vessels to receive the sacrament of marriage. So
shall ye be joined before the God and Goddess.

The bride and groom then turn towards the altar and kneel, he on the
right side, she on the left, and the celebrant says:

Now shall you speak the solemn vows which you have
prepared to each other.

At this stage, the bride and groom can simply speak their vows from
memory, but the chances are that they will be nervous and forget them.
Alternatively, the occasion may call for something slightly more formal.
So the celebrant should have a written copy of the vows. For a more
formal occasion, he or she may say:

Do you, [name], take this woman to be your wife in the sight
of the Gods and your fellow beings.

I do.

Then repeat after me . . .

The groom repeats his vows. He can either use a published form (the Christian litany of 'For better, for worse, for richer for poorer' etc, is for example, perfectly adequate, and is a beautiful statement of 'perfect love and perfect trust') or a more personalised form, as suggested earlier. The bride should use the same form when it is her turn.

The exchange of vows is followed by the consecration of the rings, which are presented to the couple on a tray or cushion. There must be two, for the Pagan ceremony emphasizes that the couple are bonded to each other in equality. The groom places a ring on the bride's finger, and she puts one on his. If the celebrant is a priest or priestess, she or he may then formally pronounce them man and wife, placing his or her hands on their heads if they so wish:

> I, [name], priest/priestess of [name of group], do hereby pronounce you man and wife in the presence of the God and Goddess and these witnesses, and long may your union be blessed.

The celebrant, or an assistant, then ties the ankles and the wrists of the couple together, and as they remain kneeling the celebrant asks the gods for blessings, long life, joy and harmony for the couple. Then he or she lights the white candle, praying that their love may never be snuffed out, blesses them and unties them, after which they embrace and are congratulated by everyone present. Afterwards, it is a pleasant custom for the newly married couple to jump over a broomstick with all its connotations of fertility, and then the party can begin.

There are many variations on this ritual that are equally valid – the above is just one example – and which one you choose is a matter of personal taste and the wishes of those most concerned – the couple.

Death

Sadly, in our society the subject of death is still hedged about with taboos; it often remains unmentionable or is referred to in euphemisms. But it should not be so. It is part of the natural cycle and should be treated as such. Some Pagans believe that this life is the only one we have, but that like ears of corn or leaves on a tree, we are part of a greater whole. For them, the Pagan funeral rites are there to remind us all that although we must say our farewells to a dear friend, he or she will live on in us, and that every laughing memory or tale we tell will bring the person to life again, just for an instant, in our hearts.

Generally speaking, however, most Pagans accept the doctrine of reincarnation as followed in Eastern religions, whereby each soul experiences a number of lives during which it strives to perfect itself until it no longer needs to reincarnate. That is in keeping with the teachings of our Celtic forebears, who also believed that the soul lived on after death and then entered a new body. Pagans do not fear death or see it as the end of everything, but rather regard it as part of the ever-changing wheel of existence, from which we can only free ourselves by achieving a state of perfection. We do not accept the existence of somewhere called Hell, and we do not fear eternal punishment at the hands of the Devil and his minions, but we also differ from Eastern religions like Hinduism and Buddhism in that we have a different attitude towards human existence. In the East, material existence tends to be seen as a burden from which the individual longs to escape through detachment. In the West, we believe that the world has many delights to offer as well as evils, and that through our relationships with others we can come to terms with our lives.

Anyone who works through the annual seasonal festivals will instinctively understand the cyclical nature of existence into which we all are inextricably woven. Whether we are destined to die comfortably in our beds of old age or as the result of a horrific accident or debilitating illness, one thing we know is that we are a microscopic part of Nature and that we must be born, mature and die, and then be reborn again. But we must still acknowledge that our dead friends have gone. The Greeks also believed in reincarnation, but only after the soul had drunk from Lethe, the river of forgetfulness. The soul may live on, but the chances are that we will not see the mundane aspects of our departed friends again. Everything that made them human – their memories, their habits and their behaviour – will be lost. Everything that makes them divine – their capacity for love, their will to live, their compassion for others – will remain and return.

The most obvious ritual in connection with death, of course, is the funeral service. Everyone should leave clear instructions about this if they wish it to be a Pagan ceremony, not only so that those who are left behind know what they are doing, but also to pre-empt any attempts by non-Pagan next of kin to hold a service which is in their eyes more traditional. Possibly, as more families grow up as Pagans, this will become less of an issue, but many funerals can become a shoddy compromise between, for example, Christian family and Pagan friends. In such cases, it is possible to come to some arrangement, perhaps for two separate ceremonies, but do be tactful. The non-Pagan contingent will be hurting just as much as you, and this is a time to show that Pagans can accept and incorporate the tradition of other religions.

Anyone can conduct a funeral for a friend at a municipal crematorium, as such establishments cater for all faiths. The only requirement is that the words of committal must be spoken, to signal to the person responsible that the curtain should be closed on the coffin. Apart from that, there is no set ritual for a Pagan funeral. The celebrant, who is often a personal friend nominated by the deceased, needs to prepare something suitable, always bearing in mind the sensibilities of the mourners, who may well be distressed or simply embarrassed. The Pagan Hospice and Funeral Trust is a good place to ask for advice on planning a funeral, and the Pagan Federation keeps a list of priests and priestesses who are happy to officiate.

If you want a Pagan funeral you should provide clear instructions and deposit them in a safe place together with your will, as your next of kin may not necessarily know what to do. If you have close Pagan friends or are a member of a worshipping community, you will probably have someone in mind to officiate; if so, his or her address and telephone number should be given. Any particular choice of music should be listed, together with instructions concerning the disposal of any magic items, ritual jewellery and robes that you may have. Some traditions require that anything of that nature should be physically destroyed or buried, but if not, you may prefer such treasures to be left to their family and friends.

A funeral service generally lasts about twenty minutes, and as the next group may be waiting outside, the person officiating must be sure not to overrun. Depending on the beliefs of the deceased, it can be as secular or religious as you want. What is actually said must of necessity depend upon the mourners, who may well include family members, non-Pagan friends, neighbours and even colleagues from work, but in general terms it is customary to start with a brief statement about how Pagans regard death, bearing in mind that the purpose of the ceremony is to give comfort to the bereaved. This should be followed by some details of the life and character of the deceased, and then perhaps by readings from a favourite book or poem and a prayer or prayers for the ease of his or her onward journey. The final stage is the actual committal, which could be as follows:

> We commit the spirit of our beloved friend, [name], into the care of the great Mother, to whom we shall all return in due course and who will give us comfort and rest in her blessed realms.

Alternatively, there is the following turn of phrase, which Anthony Kemp heard at a recent funeral:

> Into the loving embrace of the great Goddess, mother of all life, we commit the soul of our beloved brother, [name]. Free of earthly bonds, may he rest in the sunlit Lands of the West, finding peace with our ancestors, finding peace, and loving comfort to refresh him before his onward journey. Blessed be and fare thee well.

If a priest or priestess is officiating he or she may consider it appropriate to bless the mourners before they depart.

In *Eight Sabbats for Witches* the Farrars have published a ritual which they call Requiem. Essentially this is for use within a coven as a farewell for a member, and is thus what we might term a memorial service. We will all be confronted at various times by the death of family members or special friends who may well not have regarded themselves as Pagans. In such cases, in addition to the funeral service, which we may or may not attend, we may wish to mark their passing with our own private requiem, either alone or in the company of Pagan friends. The following ritual is offered as a suggestion for marking the passing of someone you were close to. It is not, of course obligatory, and should only be worked if you feel the need, but it can be a genuine comfort in time of loss, and help you to cope with bereavement.

At the chosen time, prepare the temple and bath and robe yourself as usual. Place a new unlit white candle on the altar and choose some music, if possible a piece that was a favourite of the person you are remembering. After opening your circle, switch on the music and meditate about the person, concentrating on the happier times. Imagine your friend laughing and healthy, and remember shared moments of merriment as well as sadness. When you feel ready, light the new candle and say something along the lines of the following invocation as you stare into the flame:

> [Name] has departed from this incarnation but lives on in this flame as a bright star in my memory. She/he has left to dwell in the blessed realm of the Summerlands, the land in the west where she/he will be granted rest and refreshment before being reborn again. Ancient Goddess Hecate, comforter of the dying, receive [name] into your arms and give him/her your blessed peace and comfort. May she/he there be reunited with those who have gone before. For we know that when refreshed and rested amongst our dear ones, we will be reborn again through the grace of the great Mother who never dies. Lady, I thank you for the knowledge and love of [name] and I entreat that when my time comes, I may meet, know, remember and love him/her again.

After the invocation, listen to some more music or read from a work that your friend particularly loved, which could be something humorous or light-hearted – Pagans celebrate the vibrancy of life. Take a cup of wine and drink to your friend, feeling that she or he is there to drink it with you, but do not forget to leave some for the Earth afterwards. Again, when you feel you are ready, say the following farewell:

> As the flame of the candle burns, so shall the blessed memory of [name] live on in my consciousness. Fare you well as you cross the Rainbow Bridge, over the dark chasm and into the eternal light of the gods among whom you will dwell. There shall you dance in the meadows and drink of the pure waters of knowledge. There shall you dwell in the Golden Temple and hear the music of the gods at the end of time. Great Lady, Hecate, into thy hands I commend the spirit of [name], knowing that she/he will be made whole again. Blessed be, dear friend, and may your repose be sweet.

Close down the temple and, assuming the usual safety precautions, leave the candle to burn itself out.

A requiem is an intensely private matter, and any words you use may well be dictated by the circumstances of death and the age of the deceased. Anthony Kemp once said a personal farewell to a young female friend who was dying of AIDS, more or less alone. She was asleep in a hospital bed with a dim light burning, and as he stood there that evening, he sensed that her life was ebbing away. What he whispered was intuitive, dictated by the Goddess and not part of any prepared script. When she finally died, she was virtually disowned by her family, who had her despatched without ceremony in the local crematorium, and with nobody to speak words of comfort on her behalf.

Perhaps more important than the form of the funeral ceremony is the preparation for death itself, and this has received scant attention in Pagan circles, mainly because of the relative youthfulness of the current Pagan community. However, as the population within the tradition ages and we find ourselves with a normal spread of generations, we will all begin to be confronted by the death or impending death of a friend or a family member. There is a general human tendency to fear the unknown, and it is then that we may be called upon to give comfort and hope, and even perhaps to hear a form of confession, as the person concerned may well wish to put matters right with themselves or others. This is something that requires humility and the ability to give love, consolation and absolute trust.

Neolithic tribes often laid out their dead on a bed of flowers, and in a poignant article in a recent edition of the newsletter of the Pagan Hospice and Funeral Trust, a young woman wrote about the experience of helping to dress the body of a friend in her robes before burial. When our time comes we should look forward to the next stage of our being, of meeting once again those who have gone on before, of having to face up to things we have done wrong during this incarnation and then resting for a while. At the same time, we should hope that our friends will have a splendid party after the funeral, for which, perhaps, we should leave a sum of money to ensure we are waved off in style.

Handpartings

There is another kind of farewell which is less appealing, not because of its finality but because it involves the exorcism of a bad influence from your life. There is an old Eastern saying that even if you merely find yourself next to somebody drinking from the same stream, you are probably linked to them by ties from a past life. The people you know and love may well be souls you have known and loved in previous incarnations, but there may also be people from whose influence you have to free yourself – spiteful acquaintances, destructive lovers or just plain annoying people. Remember that the Rede also applies to yourself – if a relationship is harming you, then you should put an end to it.

We have mixed feelings about Pagan divorce, because the way one looks at divorce depends on how one defines marriage. Some arrangements may be temporary, rather like betrothals or trial runs, perhaps for a year and a day, as in some Wiccan groups. But these are not true marriages. A true marriage should be entered into for life, in the Christian manner, 'for richer for poorer, for better for worse, till death do you part' – although in the Pagan tradition you may encounter each other again in the next life. It should not be a convenient way of getting what you want from the other person before unceremoniously dumping him or her and heading off for a new conquest. Live together by all means, try a temporary arrangement, but do not call it marriage unless you really appreciate what marriage is. It is one of the ultimate achievements of human life: the symbolic union (or reunion) of the two halves of God and Goddess in a sacred pair. It should not be entered into lightly, and Pagan marriage should not be seen as a soft option compared to other religions.

However, we must accept that sometimes things will go wrong. We can but hope and pray that incompatible couples can be talked out of marriage before they commit themselves for ever, and this is just one of the many advantages of the Pagan commitment to an attachment for a year and a day before making the final decision. But some people may still make the wrong decision, and since Paganism is prepared to let us make our own mistakes, it should also be prepared to help rectify them.

A Pagan divorce should take a form something like the following. The congregation should gather in the sacred space and the candles should be consecrated in an anticlockwise order to denote expulsion. The celebrant should say:

> Blessed friends, we have gathered together in this sacred place to mourn the passing of the marriage between this woman, [name], and this man, [name]. They kneel before us bound in sacred bonds, from which they wish to free themselves, in perfect love and perfect trust, though the sacred marriage was not meant to be.

The celebrant then asks each of the participants if they are willing to sever the sacred ties that bind them together. Assuming an answer in the affirmative (both participants must agree to the divorce, as both must agree to the marriage), the celebrant takes a ceremonial knife or pair of scissors and slices the ties that bind them:

> Thus I cut the bonds that bind [name] to [name], thus I free you both from the promises you have made, thus I free you to live your lives anew.

The celebrant then holds two ceremonial candles (symbolizing the bride and groom) before them and invites them to extinguish the flames, each saying:

> Hail and farewell, former wife/husband, I wish you happiness and love.

The candles are then taken to opposite sides of the sacred space and relit by the participants, he lighting hers and she lighting his. The celebrant then addresses the congregation:

> As life dies so is life reborn, as love perishes, so it flourishes anew, bear witness to the love and trust with which [name] and [name] begin their parting of the ways. Bear witness to their promises of goodwill and love, even beyond the marriage they have dissolved. Let us wait in silence as we mourn the marriage that has died, and reflect upon the future that has been reborn.

A moment's silence then begins, as the participants reflect upon the ritual that has just been performed. The sacred space should then be dissolved, and the congregation should run to embrace and congratulate both participants, in perfect love and perfect trust, as always.

The purpose of the ritual is not merely to end the marriage symbolically (it will probably have ended already in all but name), but to remind the participants and the congregation that the parting need not be bitter and recriminatory. They tried, they failed, but they have retained some dignity in the service itself. Whatever the reason for the divorce, whoever's 'fault' it may have been, they have enough humanity within them to meet one last time for the ceremonial parting. The real purpose of the ceremony is an open secret: by making the participants face each other one more time, and bringing the families together one more time, it is hoped that their co-operation and mutual understanding will foster more meetings, more friendships and general amity. It is worth a try.

Banishments

An equally distressing ritual is that of banishment, where an individual is removed from a coven, or perhaps from your life. It may be an acquaintance or ex-lover who has wronged you, or a coven member who has betrayed the others in the group.

The ritual of banishment is *not* a curse. It does not bring bad luck upon the banished, or force him or her to come cowering in search of forgiveness. It is a ritual way of excising people from your life, like cutting them out of photographs or crossing them off the Christmas card list. It is not for their benefit, but even less is it for their harm. The only person it will affect is you yourself, and the only way it will affect you is by removing that person's image from your life. It is not a quest for vengeance or a final rebuke; in fact, if you perform the ritual properly you will never think of the person again. The idea is to exorcise the bad feelings you have from your own soul, to let go of any hatred or envy you may feel and get on with your life. In other words, you will stop bearing a grudge, stop thinking of things you should or should not have said, and you will not do the individual the honour of hating him or her.

Consecrate your sacred space in the usual way, and place a solitary candle to represent the person to be banished in the centre. If there are other people present, they should begin by concentrating on their memories of the person, looking back into their minds to the occasion when they first met. What would have happened if they had never met? Can you imagine it? Would you have lost a mutual friend? Would your life have been different? If you cannot imagine life without the person, perhaps you should not be banishing him or her just yet. Maybe there is a chance of reconciliation. If there is, now is the time to speak up. The celebrant then says:

> My/our perfect love and perfect trust has been betrayed by [name], whose name shall soon be gone from sight and mind. His/her face shall not be seen, his/her voice shall not be heard, his/her touch shall not be felt. By the God and Goddess who watch over us/me, I/we purge [name] from my/our life and prepare to start anew. [Name] is gone, she/he shall not

return, it is as if she/he never was. Thrice now I/we call upon the God and Goddess, banished be she/he, banished be she/he, banished be she/he, and it shall be.

With these words, blow out the symbolic candle, and wait in silence as the smoke slowly fades away into nothingness. At that moment, the person is gone, obviously not literally from the world, but from the group. She or he cannot again come into the sacred circle, and should never be discussed, whether with good memories or bad. The banished person is gone, gone in every aspect, good and bad, and you should not accept gifts or favours and avoid any conversation or meeting. If that sounds a little harsh, remember that this is a ritual of banishment, not a little fun to help you cool down after an argument. It is final and binding, and should not be entered into lightly. A banished member could in theory enter the group again, but only with a new name, and, hopefully, a new attitude.

12 Paganism and Sexuality

The subject of sex is one of the most frequently raised topics when Paganism is discussed, and also the one that provokes the most misunderstandings, especially from the tabloid media who are ever eager for a new sensation. Gerald Gardner liked to claim that his Wicca was a fertility religion, and already in this book there have been several references to male–female polarity. Where Paganism differs from the monotheistic and patriarchal religions is that it does not come with an in-built system of taboos and has a healthy, open attitude to the human body and all its functions, including the most important one. We celebrate the beauty of the human body as a temple in which the vital spark of the deity dwells, whether fat, thin, tall, short, black or white, and there is no part of us that is not of the gods. The Pagans do not ritually scar each other, and many regard ritual circumcision, for example, as a form of legalized child abuse.

Child abuse, of course, has on occasion been mentioned in connection with 'witchcraft' by fundamentalist Christian organizations who have managed to infiltrate social work authorities in a number of places. All the alleged cases of 'ritual abuse', such as the one brought on by the scandalous behaviour of officials in the Orkney Islands, have been thrown out by the courts, and an official Home Office report has confirmed that they were totally without foundation, but only after the lives of numerous children and their families were irreparably damaged. The worst child sex abusers, sadly, are often those placed in authority over vulnerable little souls, and often people appointed by Christian organizations.

So how does Paganism view sex? As we are not hampered by an overemphasis on sin and believe our sexuality to be a gift of the gods, it follows that Pagans can take pleasure in expressing themselves sexually, but within the moral confines of the basic law: 'Do what you will, if it harm none.' There is no commandment such as 'Thou shalt not commit adultery', but the Rede is clear: you should not cause harm to your spouse by being unfaithful, if such an act would indeed harm him or her. Sex and religion are inextricably intertwined, and at the dawn of human consciousness, so-called primitive religions drew up patterns of belief based around fertility, both human and animal, which was vital for the survival of the tribe, clan or family. The female Goddess required a consort God to quicken her with life in spring as she evolved through the year as the virgin maid, the fecund mother and the old wise woman. Thus in the autumn the God had to die, only to be reborn again in celebration of the turning of the cycle of the seasons. Sexuality was also celebrated in the worship of the maleness of the bull, the stag, the ram and the hare. In the ancient world, a god of fertility was portrayed with a rampantly erect penis; nobody ever dreamed of using fig leaves to cover it. Hindus worship the male and female genital organs as the yoni or vulva of the Goddess and the lingam or penis of the God. Modern Pagans see that as completely natural, as they too worship the horned God of the wild.

The Sacred Marriage

In the earliest times, the emphasis in many rituals was sexual, and archaeologists have discovered figurines with exaggerated genitalia from the remains of many prehistoric societies and cultures. In the days when the Goddess ruled, the people doubtless had a great communal rut in the fields in her honour every spring before the planting began. The best hunter would have the pick of the available women, as it was believed that his seed would beget more successful hunters through sympathetic magic. As religions became more sophisticated, so their sexual emphasis became more formalized and structured. The pharaohs of ancient Egypt and the priest-kings of Assyria became identified with the fertility of their realms, and the concept of the *heiros gamos* or sacred marriage became a central part of the annual ritual observations in the great temples. In this, the ruler took on the role of the God, with a chosen priestess as the Goddess, and enacted the mystery of the sexual union in a ritual of sympathetic magic to prove his potency. This was seen as a magical act, and it is from this that many occult groups have derived the tradition of sexual magic.

To the pious Jews of the Old Testament, however, such lewd goings-on were anathema, as were the sins of Sodom. As a monotheistic religion anchored on the rock of patriarchy, they regarded the sole justification for sex as the begetting of children, preferably male, and were horrified by the nakedness and open homosexuality of the Pagan Greeks. Christianity took on most of the sexual taboos of the Jews, and in addition forced celibacy on the priesthood. It is only patriarchal religions that prize virginity, and that regard the deflowering of a virgin as an act of possession.

Openness about sexuality is a relatively modern phenomenon which can be dated back to the 'swinging sixties', the hippie culture and the general revolt of the youth against the outdated values imposed by parents, teachers and religions. But Aleister Crowley had practised sex magic with great enthusiasm during the 1920s, although in his writings he frequently used obscure wording to disguise his real meaning. He was obviously aware, through his extensive reading about the occult tradition, of the magical uses of sex, and was probably the source of Gerald Gardner's interest in the subject. Gardner himself had a reputation as a voyeur, and he introduced what he called the Great Rite, which entailed ritual intercourse between the high priest (i.e. Gardner himself) and the high priestess as part of the celebrations of the great festivals or Sabbats. He did specify, however, that this rite should take place in private, and the rest of the coven had to leave the room. This was in fact a reintroduction of the sacred marriage, which he also included in his pattern of initiation, as discussed in Chapter 13. Wicca is overtly sexual and some fringe covens use that as a means of gratification, but in a well-balanced and mature group the sexual emphasis is handled with responsibility and does not degenerate into a general 'gang-bang'.

In the wider Pagan community, sex is regarded as a matter for each individual, but as many people have been influenced by Wicca, it follows that there is much use of sexual symbolism in rituals, and some groups may teach sex magic. Nobody, however, should ever be compelled to take part in any form of sexual activity as a condition of membership of a hearth, lodge, coven or other group. Pagans accept the sanctity of the sexual union and realize the potency of the energies released at orgasm, the harnessing of which is the basis of sex magic. For a full, frank and beautifully written practical discussion of the subject by someone who fully comprehends it, you are recommended to read Dolores Ashcroft-Nowicki's *The Tree of Ecstasy*, which includes a series of rituals designed for a couple to work together.

Pagan couples should consider celebrating the sacred marriage once a year as a ritual to promote the fertility of the Earth and to welcome the spring. If they are married they can also use the rite as a reaffirmation of their commitment to each other. In an ideal world, it should be celebrated out of doors on a moonlit night in a woodland glade or on a freshly ploughed field before it has been sown with a crop, as a true marriage to the land, but as the weather is so inclement in many northern countries, you might try the ritual outlined below in an indoor temple space. Of course you can make love outdoors whenever the situation seems suitable, as all acts of love are in worship of the gods, and you do not always have to take your clothes off.

This ritual is suggested simply as a framework, not as a teaching. Like all magic, it can work at various levels, according to the skill of the participants at handling the energies raised. It is not just another chance to 'have a bonk', but a ritual act of worship of the moon Goddess by her male consort, the forest God. In other words, the participants must take on the role of the Goddess and the God in their minds and in their bodies. Each needs to be able to visualize the other as the deity, and to be able to hold the visualizations in their minds throughout. The naked priestess on the altar, the beloved theme of Dennis Wheatley novels, is not *on* it; she *is* the actual consecrated altar, the Goddess incarnate in woman. A couple who live together should consider a period of sexual abstinence, perhaps for a whole moon cycle, before the ritual so that when they come to it they are fresh and can bring a renewed sense of wonder to their lovemaking. Few words are included, and it is assumed that the people involved know each other well enough not to need many directions. This is one ritual which need not be worked with a set script.

You should choose a time when neither of you has to work, preferably the night of a full moon, and spend the day relaxing. A bridal bed should be prepared in the centre of the temple space. It can be an actual bed or a blanket covered with a fresh white sheet on the floor, placed so that the bride will lie with her head to the north and her legs to the south, from whence the quickening fire will enter her. Place a square of cloth underneath where the bride's genital area will be in order to catch any of the fluids that will be generated. For the altar you will need some anointing oil, ready consecrated; it should not be perfumed as the essential oil can have a very bitter taste, as well as being a possible irritant. Fill the room with flowers, have plenty of candles handy, and make sure everything is both clean and warm. Prepare something tasty to share afterwards: a bowl of your favourite fruit or some luxury like smoked salmon sandwiches, and make sure there is an open bottle of wine.

However, since your minds need to be able to concentrate, the alcohol is best left for later.

When everything is ready, you should bathe separately, as you should not see each other before you meet in the bridal chamber. The bride should wear a robe or dress that can be easily removed downwards, as well as all her ritual jewellery. The groom should preferably be dressed in a cloak or other garment that also comes off without a great deal of tugging and fumbling. In addition he should carry his sword, knife or wand if he has one, as the symbol of his maleness.

When she is ready, the bride walks into the temple and consecrates the sacred space, after which she should spend some time quietly meditating on the virgin Goddess and sensing the power within her body, pulling silvery light into herself. The groom should wait in another room but remain within earshot, waiting for the summons from the Lady. He should meditate on the God power that is within him, smelling the forest and the wildness of his nature, concentrating on his manhood and his love for the Lady. The bride should then invoke the presence of the God out loud, facing the altar and not glancing behind her, using such words as:

I am the Goddess who dwells within [own name], the power of moon and stars, the eternal mystery. But lo, I am incomplete and I yearn for my consort, the wild forest Lord who cares for my creation. Mighty Lord, I do summon thee to come forth from thy secret places, that I may know thee again. Come Lord, come unto me. . . .

When he hears these words, the groom should walk silently into the temple and stand just behind the bride, so that she can feel his breath upon her hair and neck as their auras touch. Both should consciously feel the mingling of their auras and hold this thought for a while as they feel the excitement and anticipation build. Then he should whisper gentle words of love to her and slowly turn her around so that they are facing, as if seeing each other for the first time. He will then kneel before the Lady and place his sword or wand, if he has one, at her feet, symbolically laying his power before her as he worships her as the Goddess incarnate. She should then say:

Only if thou art the true God mayst thou unveil me, as no mortal man may gaze upon my nakedness and live.

He will affirm that he is the true God, and disrobe his Lady slowly and with deliberation, gradually uncovering her body as he lowers her garment to the floor, eventually kneeling once more before her. Then he will lovingly kiss her feet, knees, womanhood, breasts, lips and fore-head, the seat of the third-eye chakra that controls clairvoyance, gradu-ally rising as he does so. The action is repeated as he takes the oil and anoints her on the same places, gently stimulating her body at the same time. The bride then disrobes the groom, kissing and anointing his feet, knees, scrotum, the stem and tip of his penis, his belly, chest, lips and forehead. Thus both are consecrated and they should stand with arms and legs wide apart and examine each other with wonder and delight. She should see his manhood as a shining jewelled sword, and he should see her womanhood as a jewel-encrusted cup, the chalice, the cauldron of Cerridwen and of rebirth.

They then lovingly embrace each other, and he tenderly lowers her on to the bed, on which she should lie with her arms and legs outstretched and the square of cloth carefully located beneath her womanhood. The so-called missionary position is by no means manda-tory; if it is preferred she can kneel so that the stag Lord penetrates her from behind as he would a doe. This is cool, loving sex, so the groom should then caress the secret places of the body of his Lady, and she should caress him in the same way, whispering loving words, until they feel ready for the final act. By then they should have entered into their roles as Goddess and God fully, with all their senses racing in anticipa-tion of their sacred union. The groom should then place himself so that he is kneeling between the outstretched legs of his bride, gazing upon the chalice that is her womanhood, and she should see his erect penis as the wand that will fill her cup with new life. He should then offer a suit-able invocation such as the one below.

O blessed Lady, eternal and divine, Goddess of the bright
    moon,
Open up thy secret pathways, that I may partake of the
    communion of the senses.
Let thy overflowing stream guide me to the mystery.
Grant that my seed may blossom within thee,
And that our love may quicken all of creation.

The actual penetration should be slow and deliberate, and then both should lie without moving for a while, harmonizing their breathing and sensing themselves as one living organism surrounded by an aura of bright silvery light like a cocoon, suspended in time. They must hold the visualization of themselves as God and Goddess with the wand embedded in the chalice before they start to move. The aim is to create a gradual progress towards the eventual climax of their orgasm, which should be mutual if at all possible. As the climax comes and the sperm pours forth, they should both visualize their cocoon of light spreading outwards from their bodies to cover the fields, forests and all the wild places with light and love.

When they separate, they should give each other the sacred communion by each dipping a finger into the vagina and placing a drop of the intermingled fluids on the other's tongue. They should also place a drop within the chalice of the wine, to mingle the drink they share. Then the bride should take the square of cloth and carefully wipe any trace of fluid from her own genitals and from the groom's penis, before reverently folding it and carefully placing it on the altar. At some later stage this should be taken out into a wild place and lovingly buried as an offering to the Earth Mother, together with a prayer for fertility. The bride and groom can linger in the temple, naked and relaxed, and should take some food and wine to give them strength before invoking the deities to depart and closing their sacred space. Afterwards, in their own bed, they should make love again as a humble man and woman, to earth themselves.

Other Acts of Pagan Sexuality

The above is a basic ritual that can be adapted for other suitable occasions, such as when a couple wish to conceive a child. They can choose an ideal date based upon astrological observations, or as the result of a divination chart they have prepared. The rite can also be used as a powerful means of raising energy to cast a spell, in which case the couple have to be able to concentrate upon the object of the spell and the desired outcome. Although it is a logical rite to celebrate at Beltane, it can be adapted for use at Lugnasadh as well, when the corn king is ritually slain. In that case it is the man who is the altar and the Goddess comes down upon him before ritually making a cut to shed his blood on to the land.

Not everybody has a partner, either by choice or circumstance, but sexual energy can also be harnessed by masturbation if that is felt to be desirable. A lone man can still ritually offer his sperm to the Earth as a fertility ritual in spring, and a woman can lie, imagining the Sun God entering her as she masturbates, holding the same visualization and offering her fluid.

Although some Pagan groups are homophobic, it should be pointed out that the sacred marriage is a symbolic union of principles. The man and woman are not physical incarnations of the God and Goddess, but spiritual ones, united in perfect love and perfect trust. In theory, then, the ritual may also be performed by same-sex couples, with one enacting the role of the Goddess and the other the role of the God. Some Pagan circles do not accept this, claiming that homosexuals would jeopardize the male–female polarity of a particular group, and that their lovemaking is contrary to Nature's commandments, but we would remind them that Nature 'commands' nothing, save that we do as we will, if it harms none. We all have the right to express our sexuality in whatever way we please, and what consenting adults do in the privacy of their own homes is their own affair. There are groups catering for homosexual and bisexual folk that advertise in the Pagan press, and we know of a heterosexual priestess who runs a highly successful hearth consisting entirely of gay folk, both men and women. However, what does grate somewhat with us is the institutionalization of exclusivity, be it hetero- or homosexual. Some Dianic covens, for example, are merely repeating the age-old errors of Christianity, but by excluding men instead of women.

Pagans see sex as a sacred matter which should not be abused, but nor should it be suppressed for the sake of religious taboos. It is regarded as completely natural and is something to be enjoyed by responsible folk. Our bodies are temples in which the deities dwell, and thus all parts of them are holy. If some of us like to take off our clothes and join our friends in dancing around an oak tree in the moonlight, why not? Pagans abuse neither their children nor themselves, but enjoy a religion that grants them freedom from the taboos imposed by men.

13   Initiation and Priesthood

Initiation

One question frequently asked of Pagans is whether one needs to be initiated, and if so, who does the initiating. The simple answer is that initiation is not as necessary as many groups would have us believe. Many good Pagan folk have never been initiated into anything and have no desire to be, but this certainly does not mean that they have a lesser status. Some traditions, however, especially Wicca, are initiatory in character, and as this book is a general introduction to Paganism, it is worth considering the matter.

The dictionary definition of initiation is: 'Ritual transition from one status to another, as from childhood to adulthood, with attendant ceremonies and ordeals. A dominant theme is the symbolism of death and rebirth. Testing the initiate's worthiness to enter the new status, it often involves special instructions, restrictions, seclusion and/or mutilation. Among the most important social institutions of traditional, preliterate societies, it continues in such modern contexts as fraternal orders and secret societies.'

In tribal societies, the rites at puberty are initiatory in character, in that they are often carried out in secret and usually involve testing the candidate's stamina through the infliction of pain. Whipping, branding, scarring and circumcision feature in such ceremonies as well as such refinements as seclusion in a dark place to encourage in the candidate a sensation of extreme terror. In more sophisticated societies in the ancient world, the crueller aspects fell into abeyance and were replaced by complicated rituals which certain adults were able to undergo. The so-called mystery cults in classical Greece were only open to those who had been initiated into them and candidates were sworn to secrecy about the

181

nature of the experience, which is the main reason why we know so little about them. In the well-known book *The Golden Ass*, Lucius Apuleius does go into some detail about his initiation as a priest of Isis, a cult which spread into Greece and Rome from Egypt and became hugely popular. Another indication can be found in a series of frescoes that have been preserved in one of the villas at Pompeii, which show an initiation into the Orphic mysteries. A young girl is prepared as a bride to indicate that she will marry the god, and as a symbolic death before rebirth she undergoes scourging. In the final scene she is shown naked, dancing ecstatically to denote that she has been reborn as a consort of the god.

The best-known mystery cult was that of Demeter and Persephone at Eleusis, which lasted more than a thousand years and attracted thousands of candidates annually. The goddess Demeter journeyed into the underworld to rescue her daughter Persephone, who had been abducted by Hades, the Dark Lord. The initiation rituals of the Eleusinian mysteries lasted for several days, but their precise nature has never been reliably revealed. The initiate entered the temple at nightfall, when it was dark without as well as within. There would have been a frisson of fear at the unknown and we know that something was revealed, something was done, and something further was revealed. What the candidates received was said to be a blessed afterlife after having participated in the rites of the goddess. In mundane terms, what they received may have been no more than membership of an exclusive club, analogous to the Freemasons, a political party or a gentlemen's drinking club, whose members had friends in high places, and whose initiation ritual served to bind the disparate initiates together. No one knows whether something mysterious was really revealed or whether the participants just engaged in some bizarre ceremony, so disgusting that the knowledge of their deeds would forever have to be kept secret, thereby making them mutually dependent on the silence of their colleagues. Whatever went on in the Eleusinian mysteries, the cult was as well known and as little understood in its day as Freemasonry and Rosicrucianism are in modern times.

When Gerald Gardner introduced Wicca he specified that as well as being a fertility religion it was also a mystical one, and laid down a system of three degrees of initiation. Since Gardner was also a Freemason, he may have copied these from them. A number of contemporary Pagan groups which no longer adhere strictly to the tradition of Gardnerian Wicca have nevertheless retained their initiatory character by adopting Gardner's rituals, shorn of their fake medieval language, or have made up similar ceremonies to suit their own needs. Some of the Nordic traditions are initiatory, as are most lodges of ceremonial magicians. Where initiation is practised, it can either simply confer membership of an organization or be a genuine mystical experience. The problem is that the difference between the two depends on the quality of the initiators, which cannot be judged in advance. In an ideal world, they should be completely trustworthy and act as conduits for the energies which the candidate will experience, because a true initiation takes place on a different plane, and can affect individual initiates in different ways.

In Chapter 3 we give a ritual of self-dedication as a Pagan, but beyond that some people feel the need to go through an initiatory process in order to experience the mysteries, a need that is as old as time itself. It is possible to initiate oneself in the sense that through trance and meditation, one can experience the totality of vision that leads to knowledge of the deity. But of course, even in the Eastern traditions where such a solitary pursuit of enlightenment is widespread, there are also groups and societies which teach the early stages of the path towards nirvana. Some Shamanic traditions teach how to achieve that experience through hallucinogens, drumming and chanting, thus entering into an altered state of consciousness. Almost all of us who are seeking something beyond mundane existence have probably experienced blinding flashes of vision at some time or other, and these in themselves can be initiatory. A sudden insight or a moment of realization, known as *satori* in Zen, is by no means unknown in Paganism, and many of today's well-known Pagan figures are self-initiated in the sense that they have never felt the need to join any particular group and thus undergo its initiation rituals.

But of course you cannot initiate yourself in the sense of making yourself a member of an organization, and if you do become part of a Pagan group, you may be initiated into various levels of its hierarchy and should expect the initiation to perform several functions. It should remind you of the importance of the vows you are making, affirming that you come to the group in search of knowledge and prepared to contribute to the well-being of both it and its members. It should recognize your willingness to abide by the laws of the group – Paganism itself has no rules, but if you join one of its denominations, you volunteer to follow its guidelines. If you do not like what you are asked to do, you should not be doing it. All initiation rituals, from all religions, have an important subtext which is often ignored: you have the chance to say no. Although it is rare for a bride to say, 'I do *not*' or a priest to say, 'Actually, I don't think I *do* believe after all', the point of the question and answer

sections of these rituals is to ask you, one final time, if you really want
to go through with it.

There is a psychological element as well, which is that the harder one
has to work for a reward, the more likely one is to appreciate it once it
is received. This is particularly relevant in secret societies such as
Freemasonry, and in old-style witchcraft when there was a heavy risk of
persecution. The initiation ceremonies were designed to instil a degree
of fear, in order to remind the participants that they were embarking on
a solemn and secret pact. Just like the yes/no questioning, the deliberate
disconcerting of the initiate in many initiation rituals is designed to
weed out those who are not yet ready to listen to the promises they are
making.

In theory, the practice of initiation should remain eternally secret, but
Janet and Stewart Farrar published the Wiccan rituals in their book *The
Witches' Way* some years ago, something about which there are mixed
feelings. Publication has largely taken away the sense of mystery that the
candidate should experience, but on the positive side, openness has
helped the growth of Pagan beliefs enormously in recent years. Vivianne
Crowley has also written about initiation in eminently sensible terms in
her book on Wicca, but wisely leaves out much of the detail of the experience itself.

In the first initiation into Wicca, the candidate meets the Goddess,
experiences a ritual death and is reborn as a priest or priestess and
witch, equipped with a new name. Depending on the capabilities of the
coven leadership, it can either be an emotive experience or be marred by
silly horseplay. The symbolism has been taken from ancient sources and
the fact that it actually works is itself a validation of the whole concept.
Candidates are first undressed and given a ritual bath as a rite of purification. The undressing stresses the removal of earthly symbols, in terms
of clothing which can denote status, so that one first approaches the
deities as naked and unprotected as a child. After the bath, they are
blindfolded, their arms are bound and their legs hobbled before entering the temple. In this adaptation of the ritual, they are laid on the floor
and covered with a dark blanket. They are then guided through a visualization of death and descent into the tomb, which leads to the rebirth
of life and eventual reincarnation as a new person. Gardner has a murky
fascination with flagellation and the candidate in Gardnerian Wicca
receives a number of strokes with a scourge made of embroidery silk,
which all seems rather pointless. This is followed by purification in the
four elements, anointing, an oath of secrecy and then the removal of the

blindfold and the release of the binding to symbolize re-emergence as a different person.

Each coven or other such group has its own rules governing admission, and most specify that a candidate must wait for a year and a day in the Outer Court. Gardner laid down a rule that only a woman may initiate a man and only a man may initiate a woman, although he made one exception – a woman may initiate her own daughter. Some covens offer a detailed training programme prior to initiation, while others simply leave the candidate completely in the dark. What is important is that if you opt at some stage for initiation you must have absolute confidence in the initiator, to the extent that you must be prepared to be stripped and bound, thus delivering yourself absolutely into his or her hands. It is a big step to take.

The second degree involves candidates in a sacred drama that re-enacts the Eleusinian legend of the descent of the Goddess into the underworld. The underlying symbolism is that candidates must encounter the dark side and the contrasexual aspect of their nature. Our own preference is to leave that as a ritual for a woman and a man, to use the slaying of the corn king at Lammas as a sacred play in which he must offer his own blood as a token sacrifice to the earth, and encounter the Dark Goddess, but there are many other religious traditions of triumph over fear and adversity. In other words, the candidate should go through a symbolic death and rebirth of some kind, as she/he leaves behind the old life and embarks on the new. The taking up of a new name, even if only among Pagan friends, is part of this process. In Wicca, the second degree of initiation confers the status of high priestess or priest, and is often conferred a year and a day after the first initiation. The use of sacred drama is an ancient feature in initiations, and if well performed can have a powerful emotional and psychic effect on candidates who take part in it.

Having encountered both light and dark, the third degree brings the two together in perfect balance through the enactment of the sacred marriage between the candidate and the initiator. Gardner ordered that the ritual could be consummated fully or 'in token'. If it was consummated fully, it should be done in private, after the rest of the coven had left the place. We discussed the sacred marriage in Chapter 12. Here it need only be said that the use of a physical act of sexual intercourse as part of an initiatory chain can cause an awful lot of problems within hearths and covens. For a start, Paganism is all about personal freedom and nobody should ever be compelled to take part in anything they find distasteful. If those involved are mature enough, however, the sacred marriage should be experienced, even if only once, in the development of someone who is following that particular path. If that most solemn ritual degenerates into an excuse for the high priest to molest the pretty young witches in his coven, then as an initiation it will be invalid. As regards celebrating the rite 'in token', this seems fairly pointless; if you are not prepared to consummate the marriage of the Goddess with the God physically, why bother at all?

In serious Pagan groups which offer initiation, candidates are properly prepared and are carefully assessed during the waiting period as to their suitability, while at the same time they can get to know those who are already working together. This is a perfectly valid path, designed to ease the novice carefully into the ways and behaviour of a particular group, and it can be extremely valuable in educating oneself about the ways of the Goddess. Other Pagan groups have their own traditions of initiation, which are not openly discussed. The rituals of the Order of Brighid, for example, would lose much of their mysterious value if their content was made public. To reveal the secrets of the initiation would rob it of its mystery and turn it into simple play-acting. It is not something to be entered into lightly, as it does change you, not in the sense that you gain instant power, but in a more subtle way, such as having a far greater sense of awareness. In our tradition, the candidate has to *ask* for initiation, as it cannot simply be given to all comers, and a strong bond of friendship inevitably forms with the initiator.

The Pagan Priesthood

By its very nature, Paganism is anarchic in terms of structure and belief, without any dogma imposed from above. One of the main attractions for many has always been the lack of a priestly hierarchy imposed as mediators between the deities and the faithful, who alone are the arbiters of worship and moral conduct. The rite of initiation into a Wiccan coven gives the title of priest or priestess to the candidate and all Wiccans regard themselves as members of a priestly caste, but in the past the secretive nature of covens and other such groups meant that those priests were very difficult to contact. Despite the general opposition to a hierarchy, however, many people felt the need for a priesthood of some kind.

When we started to explore the Path for ourselves, we discovered a large community of 'lay' Pagans (for want of a better word), especially among young people who were travellers or were involved in New Age politics and the environment. They recognized the Earth Mother as a deity, loved Nature and accepted personal responsibility for their actions, with no desire to be organized in any way. But they often needed someone to take the role of a priest in marriage ceremonies, as well as at other times. As a result, a sort of priesthood evolved of its own accord, in that the more mature members of the group were regarded as the sort of people to whom others could come to discuss their problems and seek guidance. This respect for age is itself an integral part of the early development of the priesthood, and some who had had training or had studied one of the branches of Paganism simply decided to regard themselves as priests or priestesses.

The first real priesthood, however, was the inspiration of Olivia Durdin-Robertson and her late brother Lawrence, who in 1976 founded the Fellowship of Isis (FOI), based at Clonegal Castle in Ireland and devoted to the rebirth of the worship of the Goddess throughout the world. A priesthood was re-established, based on the Durdin-Robertsons' claim to inheritance through the goddess Scota, who gave her name to Scotland. Priesthood within the FOI is conferred through ordination by a priest or priestess, and is a very moving ceremony. The candidate is given gifts, but has to offer his or her service to the Goddess in return, and at the end is formally robed before blessing the others present. Priests and priestesses are encouraged to use the title of Reverend.

You do not have to be ordained, however, to fulfil the role of priesthood, and we know of several individuals, greatly respected and admired as priestesses, who simply work through their own circle of friends and students, while others practise an open ministry. The well-known writer on Pagan mysticism, Caitlin Matthews, has even referred to herself as a 'freelance priestess'.

In comparatively recent times, the need for a priesthood has become more and more apparent as the numbers following the Pagan Path increase and they seek guidance. Leicester University has a Pagan chaplainess who is officially recognized as such, and there are a number of hospital chaplains and prison visitors. That type of ministry obviously requires a person who is prepared to fulfil a public office and to be available to all.

The role of the priest or priestess in Paganism is twofold. First, there is a deeply felt need among many folk for guidance as they step on to the Path and cannot find a spiritual haven within any one particular group or organization. The priest or priestess has to be available to offer that guidance, not as incontrovertible dogma but as sensible advice and practical help. It is not his or her job to crush or mould the seeker's own initiative, merely to provide aid when it is requested. Secondly there is the aspect of ministry, which can involve caring for someone in hospital, counselling for personal problems and celebrating rituals of birth, marriage and death for those who feel the need or lack the experience to do it for themselves. The Pagan Federation maintains a list of those prepared to conduct rites of passage and to act as prison or hospital visitors; the Pagan Hospice and Funeral Trust can provide names of members able to conduct funeral ceremonies.

The thorny problem will always be qualifications, as unlike the Christian ministry, there are no predetermined examinations, no seminaries, no hierarchies. A Pagan who claims to hold fifty different magical degrees and can quote the names of all the Hebrew archangels backwards may be highly developed spiritually but quite incompetent when it comes to offering care and comfort to someone in need. Christian priests often refer to their work as a 'calling' and the same should apply within the Pagan community; the priests should have a mission to help. That said, there are folk who quietly exercise their priesthood through prayer and meditation for the healing of the planet, rather than publicly officiating at weddings and other ceremonies.

There are many qualities which should set priestly folk aside from other Pagans. First and foremost is humility, as we are all equal in the sight of the gods. Then comes maturity, which is not determined by age but rather by outlook and experience of life – we must all suffer in order to learn. Knowledge is another vital requirement, not in the narrow sense of having detailed information about just one particular discipline, but more in the sense of having a wide and tolerant understanding of the Pagan scene in all its varieties. Another important attribute is compassion. If you were lying ill in hospital, you would like to be visited by someone who could give love, comfort and encouragement. If the person had those qualities, it would not matter at all whether he or she wore Christian robes or Buddhist ones, or was a Gardnerian high priestess, the Archdruidess of Stonehenge or a fat woman dressed up as a Viking. Lastly, Pagan priests and priestesses need plain common sense and a realization that none of us can cure the evils of the world.

People who claim to be priests or priestesses but are no good in the role will soon be found out, and their clients will vote with their feet.

Once again, Paganism's greatest weakness is also its greatest strength – while there is no ultimate authority or holy book to set down the rules, there is also no threat of retribution if you think you are sitting at the feet of a charlatan. Just get up and walk out.

The majority of Pagan clergy are women, and there are several reasons for this. The fact that Paganism acknowledges the spiritual power of women has had a powerful effect. Not only does the existence of male–female equality make Paganism more appealing to many women than the patriarchal pronouncements of Christianity, it draws in a lot of believers through its logical consequence, the male–female priesthood. A great number of spiritual women who could have worked wonders as pastors in the Christian community, have been put off by the patronizing attitude of the Church, and instead sought a role in the Pagan world. Now that Christianity is slowly dragging itself into the nineteenth century and reconsidering the role of women, it is likely that more potential Pagans will instead stay within the Christian cloisters. This is, however, rather a good thing, as the influence of increasing numbers of women in the Church cannot fail to drag it round to a very Pagan way of thinking. After a century of women bishops and increased awareness of Paganism's positive side, it may be that Paganism and Christianity will become indistinguishable.

Many religions have a higher concentration of female than male members, just as they tend to have higher concentrations of ethnic minorities and other repressed groups in search of meaning in a world dominated by white males. Paganism has even more so because of its female-friendly outlook, and this can be problematic, especially in those denominations that require equality of numbers. It can give an unfair advantage to men in some Wiccan covens, because a ritual requiring both male and female clergy may mean that the limited number of male members travel further and faster up the promotional ladder than their female colleagues, who invariably outnumber them. The upshot of this, especially in Wicca, is that the higher echelons of female clergy are extremely proficient and experienced, partly thanks to the greater competition at the lower levels, while some male priests, especially in small covens, seem to be there merely to make up the number in the rituals, since they have not put in enough time as a lower-level priest to understand the rituals, verses and ceremonies fully.

Some Pagans regard this as a minor problem, but others see it as one more reflection of the natural world. Females outnumber males in most species and most species have females who are responsible for the majority of the creative tasks. Perhaps we should welcome the fact that there are fewer men, especially in the early stages of neo-Paganism when we are still seeking to redress the balance undone by century after century of Christian oppression and patriarchal propaganda.

It is probable that in the future a Pagan priesthood will develop by a process of natural selection, simply to meet the obvious requirements of the changing times and situation. In many denominations there will never be a formal qualification or ordination, and indeed, we hope that tradition will continue. We should all maintain our rights to worship our gods in our own ways, alone or in the company of others. But those who feel the need for guidance or want someone to name and bless their children may one day be able to look up their local priestess in the Yellow Pages.

It is a very moving experience to witness a Pagan priestess in her robes and jewellery conducting a rite, as women have at last been freed to fulfil their natural, caring, spiritual role in the community. If Paganism is to be accepted alongside all the other religions, the priesthood will have a positive role to play, by setting an example as leaders and authoritative spokespeople. And if they join such bodies as local interfaith councils, the voice of Paganism will be heard in the wider community, where its ideals have much to offer in the fight against social deprivation and alienation from society.

14   Into the Future

Important dates always attract their fair share of prophecies and doom-sayers. With the coming of the new millennium we have had the usual round of cataclysmic threats and terrible harbingers of the end of the world. According to the lunatic fringe of some Christian sects, Armageddon, the final great battle between good and evil, takes place at this time. The world will be destroyed and the righteous (meaning themselves) are absorbed into heaven. However, the sects have become vaguer and vaguer about this as time goes on – the two-thousandth anniversary of the birth of Christ actually occurred several years ago, and nothing happened. But nevertheless, there are still a lot of people gullible enough to book themselves into the Jerusalem hotels ready for a front row seat of the apocalypse on New Year's Day 2001.

Pagans tend to take a slightly longer-term view, and the only 'disaster' we worry about is the attitude of so many people to the environment. If one believes that Jesus is going to return with a divine vacuum cleaner and clear up the world for all mankind, there probably is not much point in worrying about pollution and nuclear waste. But Pagans realize that if human beings continue on the present course of destruction and the world does *not* end in the near future, there will be little left of this planet but an empty shell. Therefore, we all have an obligation to work together to conserve what is left, although cynics might say that it is too late and the inherent greed of human beings will never be conquered. Paganism accepts that all things ultimately wither and die, including ourselves, but we also believe that everything is regenerated. By over-populating and ruthlessly stripping it of its natural resources, we will not cause our planet to die, although we will kill its capacity to give us life. Nowhere has the karmic cycle been more obvious.

On the face of it, politicians all over the world seem quite incapable of grasping the ecological nettle and selling the need for personal sacrifice to their electorates, in spite of the expensive conferences and the reams of paper that are produced stressing the need for the conservation of energy and natural resources. Economists still preach the creed of ever-mounting growth, but fail to grapple with the fact that such a philosophy is like a giant chain letter – somewhere down the line it must stop when the resources to promote it run out or become extinct. Many species are being hunted to extinction for the silliest of reasons, and once they are gone we will have no choice but to find alternatives. Right now, the black bears of Canada are on the brink of extinction because their claws make a fine soup for Oriental palates and their gall bladders are a traditional cure in Chinese medicine; the rest of the carcass is simply left to rot. When, in a few years' time, there are no black bears left, wealthy Chinese will have to discover a new cure, just as wealthy Arabs and Westerners will before long have to look for new fuels.

Paganism teaches love and respect for Nature in all its manifestations, and the worship and honour of the old gods, and is the natural religion of the environmental movement. As yet, this movement does not have enough voter power to force governments into positive action, but the times are gradually changing, as they have been for several decades. As the world swings into the New Age there are a number of encouraging signs. When we first became Pagans it was something to be kept quiet, something secretive. It was whispered behind the curtains of silent streets, and Pagans lived in constant fear of persecution. Legions of eager social workers waited to seize children from parents who dared admit that they were witches, and the spectre of persecution hung over every innocent suburban street. If you were a Pagan you were a witch and if you were a witch you were in league with Satan. Those who wrote for Pagan magazines tended to hide behind box numbers and pseudonyms, fearing that they might lose their jobs if it became known that they were Pagans, and telephone numbers were only divulged to close friends in case one received obscene or suggestive calls.

Now, however, things are very different, with open meetings, publicly advertised events and even attempts at dialogue between the various religions. The so-called decade of evangelism, which was inaugurated around seven years ago and declared open war upon the 'occult' does not have a target if the 'occult' is no longer 'occluded'. Members of the Pagan priesthood are now being accepted for what they are, even in some cases becoming involved in organizations such as interfaith councils. The membership of the Pagan Federation and other organizations is rising at a dramatic rate which proves, if nothing else, that Paganism is becoming increasingly attractive to more and more thinking and concerned people. Yet even now we hear remarks such as that we are a bunch of green, vegetable-hugging leftist loonies who dress up as peasants and skip through forests. True, there is a lunatic fringe, but that applies to all religions, and none is immune from the possibility of misplaced fanaticism. Religious fundamentalism and intolerance are two of the biggest menaces facing society as a whole, and yet if the only 'fundamental' was that we should not wrong another person, surely the world would be happier and more peaceful.

There are remarkably few rich Pagans, and the accumulation of wealth for its own sake is alien to the philosophy underlying the movement. An encouraging sign is that in the business world, certain people who would not necessarily describe themselves as Pagans are starting to act in a responsible way. 'Green' products, recycling and an awareness of waste and pollution are encouraging us to think about the origins of the foods and items around us, and to question whether we really need so many artificial things in our lives. Paganism is only one component of the wider ecological movement, but in the absence of any strong commitment from the established religions, it has a vital role to play in encouraging green initiatives. As Vivianne Crowley wrote in *Phoenix from the Flames*: 'The message of Paganism is to bring love, wisdom and enlightenment into manifestation in the world by returning to those things which we have lost: the wisdom of the Elder Gods.'

The general downturn of the economies of the West and the inevitable recession has led to steadily rising unemployment, among both industrial workers and managers, and, for those still in work, a desperate feeling of insecurity. Yet work is an addiction that enslaves the bulk of the population during the best years of their lives, and the basic immorality of so many business 'ethics' ruins their souls and separates them from the natural world. Politicians preach about a return to full employment and fail to tell the truth – that there will never be such a thing, as new technology is always more efficient than unionized labour forces. Many of those who are discovering the Pagan ethic come from the unemployed and what is termed the 'underclass', which is constantly rising in numbers in all industrialized countries.

So, does Paganism have any answers for the future? Yes, in the sense that the ethics of the religion and the emphasis upon respect for nature can provide a spiritual framework to fill the vacuum left by the established religions. Paganism is one antidote to the sense of spiritual deprivation experienced by ever-increasing numbers of people who are left addicted to tranquillizers and poisoned by junk food. By recognizing that we can all take responsibility for our lives, by removing the irrational fear of death and by bringing love into people's empty lives, it is a valid way forward. The new Pagans are not hippies and social misfits. They come from all backgrounds and walks of life to seek an answer for modern living within belief patterns that have stood the test of time. Non-consumerism can range from giving up work entirely to looking for less stressful forms of activity to earn the basic necessities. Many people are taking a good, long look at their lifestyle, possessions and levels of stress, and asking themselves if they really need a larger car than their neighbours, whether they could move to a house in a cheaper area with a garden for vegetable growing, and whether they could do without two salaries. Paganism has spawned a network of cottage industries, often based on the barter principle. There are also a number of Pagans who have elected to be unemployed and eke out an existence in an uncongenial atmosphere, preferring to turn their creative energies into study, art and the business of living. Anthony Kemp himself downgeared some years ago by buying a semi-ruin in the south-west of France and adopting a life of cement mixers, gardening and doing his own plumbing, which he finds infinitely preferable to a daily struggle to pay the mortgage. It was his discovery of Paganism that hastened the decision, and it is one that he does not regret. Modern technology will also enable an increasing number of people to work at home, linked to their company office by a computer network, able to set their own preferred rhythm and spend the rest of the day tending to the vegetable patch.

Paganism encourages us to make our own rules, not to mindlessly follow the herd. If you want to work all your life so that you can retire on a pittance when you are too old to enjoy having more time, that is your decision, but one of Paganism's greatest contributions is its continual, gentle reminder that life is what we make it. Work in an office, live in a farmhouse, camp on a moor, sleep on the streets; however you live your life, you will always be attached to the seasons and the Earth. Paganism helps us to affirm that bond, and remind us what we risk losing.

It is anyone's guess what will happen in the future, and the dawn of the Age of Aquarius will not be all hearts and flowers. In the media we are told of all the dangers that are in store: comets might hit the Earth; we could all get skin cancer or mad cow disease; the ice caps are going to melt and drown us; an ever-decreasing workforce will have to pay to provide welfare benefits for the rising numbers of unemployed; the ageing population will live longer on account of the advances in medical knowledge; there will be rivers of blood as immigrants flood into the industrial regions in search of a subsistence wage, stretching welfare systems further; the proliferation of sophisticated weapons coupled with Islamic fundamentalism could provoke a conflict in the world split along religious lines, a re-run of the Crusades. And for more and more young people, politics and politicians are becoming increasingly irrelevant as they observe the corruption and lack of vision in our society.

And yet none of this should matter to a Pagan. Stay out of the sun, do not eat mad cows, do not destroy the ozone layer, work to support yourself and look after your friends and family. So what if there is a comet heading towards the Earth, at last our nuclear weapons might have something productive to do with all that firepower. So what if people are living longer; the elder statesmen and women of the next few decades will be the ageing baby boomers, the love children of the sixties, the inventors of flower power. Maybe, just maybe, they will be able to bring about change through the sheer size of their 'grey' votes. And as for the immigrants, what terrors await us when we find out how other people live, and how other religions approach the world?

You cannot turn back the clock, and although there are some Pagans who prefer to live in simplicity, it would be silly to follow an Amish-style policy of spiteful hardship purely for the sake of it. The new technologies can be our friends: they are encouraging devolution of government, home rule for the Celtic realms, and greater power to the people. Secrets are harder to keep in this world of the information superhighway: politicians are not more corrupt and crime is not on the increase, it is just that more instances are being reported. We are becoming more aware of ourselves and of the changes we need to make to our society, and although it may not seem so, our voices are being heard. When the British government introduced the poll tax it proved to be uncollectable, and environmental protesters are proving that non-violent direct action can make the cost of policing anti-road demonstrations so prohibitive that contractors are increasingly unwilling to place tenders.

Whatever the future may hold, Pagan ideas will have an important role to play, and the movement's continuous evolution will ensure that it is able to cope. As more and more people flock to the cause (either as conscious Pagans or as disenchanted members of other religions who become Pagans by default) the movement will become less of an individual quest and develop into a more structured form of religious belief, relying on consensus rather than obedience to orders from a hierarchy of priests and priestesses. There are already attempts to form a loose coalition that the less well-informed on the outside will doubtless refer to as a Pagan Church. In the UK, we have the Pagan Federation, which aims to bring the disparate Pagan denominations together for understanding and the exchange of ideas. In the USA, the World Pagan Network helps to put interested parties in touch with each other. There is also the Covenant of Unitarian Universalist Pagans (CUUP), a grand-sounding name deliberately chosen to add weight to the word 'Pagan' and plant the seed with non-Pagans that Paganism should be treated on equal terms. The CUUP ensures that Pagans in the USA have a protective umbrella beneath which they can practise their beliefs. There are many other organizations, lobbies and pressure groups, some of whom are listed in Appendix 4, and each of them is striving in its own way to spread the Pagan message a little further.

Let us all work together towards an ideal of sanity for the sake of the generations to come, and bring peace, love and light into their lives. Pray to the old gods and the elemental guardians of the universe for their aid. Let them know that they are not forgotten, for this will help us to remember who we are. The monotheistic religions have had their triumphs, and now is the time to clear away their baggage and bring the world back to one truth – not a truth handed down from on high by earthly representatives, but the truth of our control over our own destiny. There is not 'One True Religion', there are six billion true religions, and new ones are being born every day. You can do whatever you want. If it harms none, do as you will.

Appendix 1
A Common Eucharistic Ritual

The desire to share food and drink in a religious setting must surely be one of the few real basics that human beings can agree on, whatever their race. The principle is as old as the religious impulse in humankind itself, bound up with the offering of fruits of the Earth to the gods and partaking of those elements, sharing in the mystic experience and giving thanks for Nature's bounty. Modern Paganism is no exception and the basic Wiccan ritual, which is most commonly used in one form or another and is sometimes referred to as Cakes and Wine, is a celebration of gender polarity with sexual overtones. Theoretically, as laid down in Gardner's *Book of Shadows*, it requires the participation of a male and a female, with the priestess using the knife (the male symbol) and the priest holding the symbolic female cup or chalice for the consecration of the wine. The consecration of pieces of cake or biscuits is then done by the priest, with the priestess reversing roles by assisting him.

The ritual works perfectly in a coven setting, but in a wider Pagan sense it can lose some of its relevance. Where people are working alone, in a non-Wiccan group or in single-sex groups, the imagery can be inappropriate. There has long been a need within the wider community of Paganism for a standard eucharistic ritual that could be embraced by all traditions, but we all know that no two Pagans can ever agree.

Aleister Crowley wrote a beautiful but highly complicated ritual known as the Gnostic Mass, which is still celebrated today from time to time, but requires several participants, including two children, one dressed in white and the other in black. The well-known writer on Celtic religion and Western mysticism, Caitlin Matthews, has also devised a ritual which she calls the Grail Mass, which is eminently suitable for general Pagan use. However, any celebration of this type throws up a wider theological issue. If a group of Pagans gather for a picnic and share their food in the sunshine, what they are doing may have a spiritual intent, but it is not a ritual as such, as the elements have not been consecrated. On the other hand, if someone assumes the role of priest or priestess and consecrates the food or wine, are they being true to themselves, or are they merely mimicking Christian practices and instituting a sacrament? In the Roman Catholic Mass, the celebrant 'empowers' the bread and wine and they are transubstantiated into the body and blood of Jesus. The rite is therefore a sacrament – a 'making-holy'. In the non-Catholic versions of Christianity, the elements remain what they are, and such rites as the Lord's Supper are non-sacramental. In the Wiccan rite, the celebrants 'empower' the elements through consecration and thus perform a magical act which is sacramental in nature (always assuming that the celebrants know what they are doing). The priestess, if she is skilled, charges the wine by pulling in astral energy and transmitting it through the blade of her knife or sword. Thus, those who partake of food and wine in a ritual setting will partake of the power within the charged elements. But that is not absolutely necessary, and it is possible that two systems will develop within Paganism, with different ritual parameters – a 'high church' and a 'low church', if you will.

There are certain occasions today when a form of religious 'service' may be required, in which non-Pagans might participate. The Feast of the Earth Mother, which is presented below is not intended as a replacement for the traditional ceremonies cherished by individuals or hearths. It could be used within a hearth on a regular basis, perhaps once a month, as part of a marriage ceremony, or when a larger number of Pagan folk (and even non-Pagans) come together to celebrate and worship. Such an occasion might be a road protest demonstration or similar environmental gathering, a music festival or a solstice ceremony. It should be possible to perform the ceremony in public without offending anyone, except for diehard fundamentalists, just as nobody ever seems to be bothered when the Druids, fully robed, perform their rites on Tower Hill. The actual working can be as simple or as complicated as the participants wish, be it with full ceremonial robes and incense, jeans and trainers at a picnic or even stark naked in the drawing room. As every one of us has the right to be a priest or priestess, this rite can be celebrated by anyone who feels able, and who is acceptable to the others present.

This version assumes a female celebrant or presider with a male assistant, and an outdoor setting such as a grassy meadow, a woodland glade or the bank of a stream. As a bare minimum, she will have a chalice of wine, mead, beer, milk or fruit juice, a plate with enough pieces of bread, preferably home-baked, for each person present, plus one extra to be returned to the Earth, a shielded candle or storm lantern and a clean cloth. A tree stump makes a suitable altar, or even a folding picnic table covered with a cloth.

A charge, a word cribbed by Gerald Gardner from Freemasonry, is a statement of principles declaimed to a candidate for initiation, or used as part of the opening ceremony in Wiccan coven workings. Also known as the Coven Charge, this particular one was written by Doreen Valiente and was included in the Gardnerian *Book of Shadows*. As it is a particularly beautiful piece of Pagan prose, and as it is used by Pagans of various persuasions, we include it as an example for more general use, with the addition of the 'cakes and wine' distribution at the end. Originally it was designed to be spoken by a high priest and a high priestess, but it can quite easily be adapted for one person.

The high priest says:

Listen to the words of the Great Mother, who of old was also called among men: Artemis, Astarte, Athena, Diana, Melusine, Aphrodite, Cerridwen, Dana, Arianrhod, Isis, Bride and by many other names.

The high priestess responds:

Whenever ye have need of anything, once in a month, and better it be when the moon is full, then shall ye assemble in some secret glade and adore the spirit of me, who is Queen of all Witcheries. There shall ye assemble, ye who are fain to learn all sorcery, yet have not won its deepest secrets; to these I will teach things that are yet unknown. And shall ye be free of slavery; and as a sign that ye really be free, ye shall be naked in your rites, and ye shall dance, sing, feast, make music and love, all in my praise. For mine is the ecstasy of the Spirit, and mine is also joy on Earth; for my law is love unto all beings. Keep pure your highest ideal; strive ever toward it; let naught stop you or turn you aside. For mine is the secret door that opens upon the land of youth, and mine is the cup of the wine of life, and mine is the cauldron of Cerridwen, who gives the gift of joy unto the hearth of man. Upon the Earth I give the knowledge of spirit eternal, and beyond death,

I give peace, rest and ecstasy, freedom and reunion with those who have gone before. Nor do I demand ought in sacrifice, for behold, I am Mother of all living things and my love is poured out upon the Earth.

Then the high priest says:

Hear ye the words of the Star Goddess, she in the dust of whose feet are the hosts of heaven, and whose body encircles the universe.

The high priestess then intones:

I who am the beauty of the green Earth and the white moon among the stars, and the mystery of the waters and the desire of the hearts of men, call unto thy soul. Arise and come into me. For I am the soul of nature who gives life to the universe. From me all things proceed and unto me all things must return, and before my face, beloved of gods and men, let thy innermost divine self be enfolded in the rapture of the infinite. Let my worship be within the heart that rejoiceth; for behold, all acts of love and pleasure are my rituals. And therefore let there be beauty and strength, power and compassion, honour and humility, mirth and reverence within you. And thou, who thinkest to seek for me, know: thy seeking and yearning shall avail thee not, unless thou knowest the mystery. That if that which thou seekest, thou findest not within thee, thou wilt never find it without thee. For behold, I have been with thee from the beginning and I am that which is attained at the end of desire.

The priest then holds out the chalice of wine, and the priestess dips the end of the knife or wand into it, saying:

Thus doth the female enter the male, thus does the male
  enter the female.
We are two united in one, there are no strangers here,
All children of the Earth are brothers and sisters.
Let us eat of these cakes and drink of this wine, that we can
  share in the bounty of our Mother.

Those attending then each take a piece of bread or cake and a sip of the wine. The final piece of bread is returned to the Earth, as are the dregs of the wine, which should be poured into the ground as a libation to the great Mother. Then the high priestess says:

> The rite is done.
> Go forth in perfect love, and perfect trust.

Appendix 2
Earth Healing Day

This is an initiative instituted by the Pagan Federation. It is celebrated on a set date each year, the idea being that a working will be all the more powerful if celebrated by a large number of people. An outline ritual is published, which is different each year, and as Earth healing is obviously of prime importance to everyone, whether Pagan or not, it can be celebrated at any suitable time, alone or in company, as it is the intention that counts. Given below is the 1996 ritual which could form the basis for a similar celebration in honour of the great Mother.

Create a sacred space in which to perform your ritual. This can be done by standing in a circle, linking hands and then attuning your energies with those of the Earth and the people around you. Call on the elements to aid your working, starting in the east.

> May the spirits of the air be with us, and let there be peace in the east.
> May the spirits of fire be with us, and let there be peace in the south.
> May the spirits of water be with us, and let there be peace in the west.
> May the spirits of earth be with us, and let there be peace in the north.
> May the Lady and the Lord be with us, bringing peace which will be felt throughout the world, for without peace there can be no healing.

The celebrant should stand quietly and feel the presence of the Lord and Lady, and of the elements. Gather them around you until you feel at one with them. The presider will explain the purpose of the gathering and start a chant or circle dance to harness the power of the place.

Close your eyes and visualize love, warmth and healing energies flowing from the Earth through you and from you, out into the world to encompass all living things. Whilst everyone concentrates, the celebrant recites:

> Gentle breeze of new-born spring,
> Sigh across the mother's face,
> Blow away all that's unclean,
> Leaving sweetness in its place.
>
> Soft spring rains shall wash her clean,
> Melting winter's frosty bite,
> Soak the stiffness from her bones,
> Leave her fertile, sparkling bright.
>
> Golden sun shall kiss her skin,
> Warming to her rosy glow,
> Swell the new seed in her womb,
> Making her spring mantle grow.
>
> (M. Graham, 1991)

At the end of the work, the celebrant instructs everyone to place their hands on the ground and feel any residual energy soak away into the ground.

All participants are handed a seed or a sapling, and the celebrant requests them to plant it with the intention that, as it grows, so will mankind's awareness of our position as guardians of the Earth. In addition, everyone should be reminded to pledge themselves, not just for a single day but for every day, to do all that they can as individuals to help the Earth heal itself. The sacred space is then dissolved. The elements, together with the Lord and Lady are thanked for their help as they depart. The following is a suggestion for a closing chant:

> Earth my body, water my blood, air my breath and fire my
>   spirit,
> The Earth is our Mother, we will take care of her.
> She changes everything she touches and everything she
>   touches changes.

However, if you know any other suitable chants, feel free to use them or make up your own.

After the ritual, it is a good idea to celebrate, have a picnic, share food and get to know others in your area, maybe even to plan future meetings with the idea of continuing the work you have started.

Appendix 3
Daily Life Upon the Path

The following essay has a mysterious origin. It was sent to Anthony Kemp several years ago in the form of an anonymous photocopy, which he then proceeded to edit, amend and add to over the course of several more years. It is included here simply because it has been sent to people in search of information about Paganism and the feedback has been extremely positive.

Having made the decision to follow the Path, which in itself is essentially a voyage of self-discovery, it cannot simply be shrugged off when inconvenient. Whether the original decision was sealed by formal initiation into a working group, a ritual of personal dedication or just a private individual commitment, a process was set in train that can never be reversed. The old gods were invoked, and whatever is done on the earthly plane sets up a corresponding vibration in the higher spheres of the subconscious. This applies equally to whatever discipline the traveller has chosen to follow: the Wiccan tradition, in its various forms, the working of ritual magic or the individualistic Pagan way, alone or in a group. All true travellers form part of a community and their journey will inevitably cast them into the company of others who may well seek to influence them, but the Path is a personal one. Its course is mapped solely by the inner guide, who is the only one whose dictates the seeker must follow.

The rule of the Path is not a written code that demands an outer conformity, but a dedication to an ideal which involves self-discipline in order that the goal may be attained. There is no merit to be obtained simply by remembering to celebrate the great festivals or to attend a monthly coven meeting. Those who follow the Path learn to accept certain ever-present spiritual principles which, as underlying cosmic

laws, govern all things. In spite of what some self-styled adepts would
have us believe, there is no 'book' in which all the great cosmic truths
are revealed, neither is there any 'guru' who can offer instant salvation.

No rules are made concerning the application of these principles to
the affairs of life; each seeker applies them to his or her own circumstances and problems, according to his or her understanding. Counsel is
not proffered unless it is asked, for until the need for guidance has been
realized, it is seldom acceptable. It is of more value that a soul should
learn to do the right thing, rather than have to be told. If the cosmic laws
are obeyed, results are obtained; if they are disregarded, there follow the
inevitable consequences of a broken natural law.

The growth of the soul takes place through many incarnations, and
different attainments are required of it in the various stages of its development. Therefore, no objective standard of achievement is set; a principle is taught, an ideal upheld, and travellers are counselled to apply
that principle and follow that ideal in the circumstances in which they
find themselves, for it is only as they are faithful over few things that
they will be entrusted with many.

Those who take the first tentative steps upon the Path often have in
the baggage they bring with them a number of notions which were
indoctrinated by parents, teachers and religious leaders. These can
include a belief in sin, the need for repentance, guilt about the enjoy-
ment of life's pleasures, and the receiving of a tangible reward for 'good'
behaviour. Yet one of the basic tenets of the Path is that we alone must
bear responsibility for our actions, as they affect both ourselves and
others. 'Do as thou wilt shall be the whole of the Law – an it harm none.'
Applying that apparently simple law to each situation as it occurs in
daily life, the traveller soon learns to become aware of cause and effect,
as well as the limitations imposed upon the exercise of his or her will.

Unlike the established religions there are no requirements for certain
exercises to be performed in return for spiritual or earthly reward. No
prayers have to be said at set times and no particular ceremonies must
be carried out regardless of one's own personal inclination at that
moment. It is the individual's own choice as to when and how often he
or she may need to ritually invoke the powers beyond us. Any such
work, however, must be carried out humbly and sincerely after due
preparation of both body and mind, otherwise it will be of no avail.

The Path is not an easy stroll through pleasant countryside, and there
are many rocky patches to be circumvented. There are also tempting
short cuts that open up to either side of the way, but these are often illu-

sory, as they lead to dead ends. Some of those the pilgrim encounters will offer the chance to stop for a while, in order to try and tempt him or her to deviate from the goal. From time to time, the Path will split in two directions, both equally valid, and the decision as to which road to take rests with the traveller.

Initiates are told that in order to learn, they must first suffer, and true seekers are not born with silver spoons in their mouths. The pilgrim setting off takes only the bare necessities needed to sustain life: the plain robe, the staff, water and food. He or she does not believe, but rather knows, that what is required will be furnished when appropriate. Over the doorway by which the initiates entered the temple at Eleusis was written: 'Know thyself.'

By taking responsibility for his or her own life, rather than leaving the rules to be formulated by others, the traveller will discover among the rocks a rich and varied scenery in which there is beauty, warmth, love and light. Although hard, the Path is ultimately one of joy and inner contentment. Walk therefore merrily with the minimum of baggage to encumber you, and may you discover perfect love and perfect trust.

Appendix 4
Useful Contacts and Information

Organizations

There are literally dozens of Pagan groups worldwide, many of which represent strictly local or specific fields of interest. The ones listed below are some of those that may appeal to a wider circle of enquirers.

UK and Ireland

The Pagan Federation
BM Box 7097
London WC1N 3XX

The leading pan-Pagan group in Britain, with extensive contacts worldwide.

The Order of Brighid
91 Reigate Road
West Worthing
Sussex BN11 5ND

A networking and friendship group with the aim of rekindling the sacred flame of Brighid of Kildare.

Hoblink
Box 1
13 Merrivale Road
Stafford ST17 9EB

A networking group for gay and bisexual Pagans.

Pagan Link
25 East Hill
Dartford
Kent

An old-established general networking circle with local contacts.

The Pagan Hospice and Funeral Trust
BM Box 3337
London WC1N 3XX

A registered charity that concerns itself with the care of the dying, death
and bereavement.

Dragon
3 Sanford Walk
New Cross
London SE14 6NB

An active eco-Pagan campaigning group.

Green Circle
PO Box 280
Maidstone
Kent ME16 0UL

A Pagan-oriented discussion forum

The Wicca Study Group
BM Deosil
London WC1N 3XX

An organization that offers training in the Wiccan tradition

Odinshof
BCM Tercel
London WC1N 3XX

Contacts with those who follow the Nordic tradition.

The Odinic Rite
BM Runic
London WC1N 3XX

Another Nordic group.

The Odinic Rite
BM Edda
London WC1N 3XX

The second of the two Odinic Rite groups in Britain.

Rune Gild UK
BM Aswynn
London WC1N 3XX

The UK outpost of a US organization, combining Heathen religion with Shamanic practices.

Hammarens Ordens Sällskap
109 Gorsedale Road
Pulton
Wallasey
Wirral L44 4AN

An eco-Heathen movement, some of whose traditions share characteristics with Zen.

The Council of British Druid Orders
125 Magyar Crescent
Nuneaton
Warwickshire CV17 4SJ

The contact address for a variety of Druidic groups.

The Order of Bards, Ovates and Druids
PO Box 1333
Lewes
Sussex BN7 3ZG

Offers postal training in various aspects of Druidism.

The Fellowship of Isis
Clonegal Castle
Enniscorthy
Ireland

A worldwide movement dedicated to Goddess worship.

USA

World Pagan Network
c/o Chris West
721 N. Hancock Avenue
Colorado Springs, CO 80903

e-mail: ceile@aol.com

Send a stamped addressed envelope or international reply coupon for a response from this volunteer organization, which will attempt to locate like-minded Pagan contacts for you in the local area.

Covenant of Unitarian Universalist Pagans
PO Box 442
Boyes Hot Springs, CA 95416

e-mail:cuups@aol.com

In a world where you do not get anything unless you are an organization, this group liaises with the Unitarian Universalist Churches to make sure that Pagans have a say and gain status as a legally recognized 'church'.

The Church of All Worlds
PO Box 212
Redwood Valley CA95470

The New Wiccan Church
PO Box 162046
MH Sacramento CA 94704

Circle
PO Box 219
Mount Harwich WI 53572

Canada

The Wiccan Church of Canada
1555 Eglinton Avenue
W. Toronto
Ont. N6E 2G9

Australia

The Pan-Pacific Pagan Alliance
PO Box A486
Sydney South
NSW 2000

Europe

Cercle du Dragon
BP 68
33034 Bordeaux
France

Eglise Druidique des Gaules
BP 13
Aubervilliers cedex
France

The Hole in the Sky
Postlager 13507
Berlin 27
Germany

Asatruarfelag
c/o Benteisson
Draghalsi
Bogarfirdi
Iceland

Paganian Europe
226024 Brivibas Street
398–104 Riga
Latvia

Romuva Vilnius
Didzioji 11
2000 Vilnius
Lithuania

Norwegian Pagan Federation
PO Box 1814
Nordnes
524 Bergen
Norway

Polish Nature Religion
vl Grodeckiego 4n 37
01–843 Warsaw
Poland

Magazines

A few years ago there were only a handful of Pagan publications, but recently there has been a great proliferation, ranging from glossy colour magazines to small photocopied newsletters put out on a members-only basis, many of which simply fade away after a few issues. The following is a selection of magazines which have stood a reasonable test of time, and most of the organizations listed above produce their own internal publications.

Pagan Dawn, the journal of the Pagan Federation (address above)
The Cauldron, M. Howard, Caemorgan Cottage, Caemorgan, Cardigan, Dyfed SA43 1QU
Quest, BCM/SCL Quest, London, WC1N 3XX
Pagan Voice, 17 Blethwyn Close, Henbury, Bristol, BS10 7BH
Greenleaf, Robin's Greenwood Gang, 96 Church Road, Redfield, Bristol 5
The Web of Wyrd, PO Box A486, Sydney South, NSW 2000, Australia.

Available in the UK from Julia Phillips, BM Box 9290, London WC1N
3XX.
Starlight, PO Box 452, 00101 Helsinki, Finland
Moira, Cercle du Dragon (address above)
Wiccan Rede, PO Box 473, Zeist, NL 3700 AL, Netherlands
Antaios, 169 Rue Washington bte 2, 1050 Bruxelles, Belgium
Circle Network News, PO Box 219, Mount Horeb, WI 53572, USA
Green Egg, Box 1542, Ukiah, CA 95482, USA

Suppliers

Five years ago, it would have been necessary to include a small list of
suppliers of Pagan needs in a book such as this but these days it seems
that every town has at least one Pagan supplier so any list here would be
unrepresentative. They may masquerade as alternative bookshops, 'head
shops' or spiritual centres, but you can be sure they are there. Many of
the magazines listed above carry lists of artists, holistic therapists, craftspeople and purveyors of incenses, hand-carved wands, statuary and so
on. One person who should be listed, however, is an excellent robe-
maker, who can supply basic patterns as well as offering a tailor-made
service for clients' original requirements. Although resident in France,
she does offer a mail order service:

Romayne Marjolin
Guerecietenia
Sise Chemin d'Ispequy
64430 St Etienne de Baigorry
France

Bibliography

Adler, M. *Drawing Down the Moon* (Beacon Press, USA, 1986)

Ashcroft-Nowicki, D. *The Tree of Ecstasy* (Aquarian Press, 1991)

Badcock, C., *The Psychoanalysis of Culture* (Basil Blackwell, 1980)

Beth, R., *Hedgewitch: A Guide to Solitary Witchcraft* (Robert Hale, 1990)

Button, J. and Bloom, W. (eds), *The Seekers' Guide: A New Age Resource Book* (Aquarian Press, 1992)

Carr-Gomm, P., *The Elements of the Druid Tradition*, (Element Books, 1991)

Chocron, D., *Healing with Crystals and Gemstones* (Samuel Weiser, 1986)

Clifton, C. (ed.), *The Modern Craft Movement* (Llewellyn, USA, 1992)

— *Modern Rites of Passage* (Llewellyn, USA, 1994)

— *Shamanism and Witchcraft* (Llewellyn, USA, 1994)

— *Living Between Two Worlds: Challenges of the Modern Witch* (Llewellyn, USA, 1996)

Collins, M., *Pagan Atheism: a Personal View* (Pagan Atheist Synthesis, 1995)

Conway, D., *Secret Wisdom* (Jonathan Cape, 1985)

Crowley, V., *Wicca* (Aquarian Press, 1989)

— *Phoenix from the Flame* (Aquarian Press, 1994)

Eliade, M., *Shamanism* (Arkana, 1989)

Farrar, J. and Farrar, S., *Eight Sabbats for Witches* (Robert Hale, 1981)

— *The Witches' Way* (Robert Hale, 1984)

Foreman, D. and Haywood, B., *Ecodefense: A Field Guide to*

Monkeywrenching, 3rd edn (Abbzug Press, USA, 1993)

Gardner, G., *Witchcraft Today* (Rider, 1954)

Green, M., *The Path Through the Labyrinth* (Element Books, 1988)

— *Natural Magic,* (Element Books, 1989)

— *A Witch Alone* (Mandala 1991)

Harding, E., *Women's Mysteries Ancient and Modern* (Shambhala, 1990)

Harris, A., 'Sacred Ecology' in Harvey, G. and Hardman, C., (eds), *Paganism Today* (Thorsons, 1995), pp. 149–56

Harvey, G., *Listening People, Speaking Earth: Contemporary Paganism* (Hurst & Co., 1997)

Hope, M., *The Psychology of Ritual* (Element Books, 1988)

— *The Psychology of Healing* (Element Books, 1989)

Hutton, R., 'The Roots of Modern Paganism', in Harvey and Hardman (eds), *Paganism Today* (Thorsons 1995), pp. 3–15.

Jones, P and Matthews, C. (eds), *Voices from the Circle* (Aquarian Press, 1990)

Jones, P., 'Pagan Theologies', in Harvey and Hardman (eds), *Paganism Today* (Thorsons, 1995), pp. 32–46.

Jones, P and Pennick, N., *A History of Pagan Europe* (Routledge, 1995)

Kelly, A., *A History of Modern Witchcraft 1939–1964* (Llewellyn, USA, 1991)

Kemp, A., *Witchcraft and Paganism Today* (Michael O'Mara, 1993)

Meadows, K., *The Medicine Way* (Element Books, 1992)

Matthews, C. (ed.), *Voices of the Goddess* (Aquarian Press, 1989)

Matthews C. and Matthews, J., *The Western Way* (Arkana, 1994)

Matthews, J., *The Arthurian Tradition* (Element Books, 1989)

— *The Celtic Shaman* (Element Books, 1991)

McCoy, E., *Inside a Witches' Coven* (Llewellyn, USA, 1997)

Peach, E., *The Tarot Workbook* (Thorsons, 1984)

Pennick, N., *Practical Magic in the Northern Tradition* (Aquarian Press, 1989)

Piggott, S., *The Druids* (Thames & Hudson, 1968)

Rees, K., 'The Tangled Skein: the Role of Myth in Paganism', in Harvey and Hardman, (eds.), *Paganism Today* (Thorsons 1995), pp. 16–31.

Sertori, J., *The Little Book of Feng Shui* (Siena, 1998)

Simes, A., 'Mercian Movements: Group Transformations and Individual Choices Amongst East Midlands Pagans', in Harvey and Hardman (eds.), *Paganism Today* (Thorsons, 1995) pp. 169–90.

Steward, R., *Celebrating the Male Mysteries* (Arkania, 1991)

Starhawk, *The Spiritual Dance* (Harper and Row, USA, 1979)

Valiente, D., *Natural Magic* (Robert Hale, 1975)

— *Witchcraft for Tomorrow* (Robert Hale, 1978)

— *The Rebirth of Witchcraft* (Robert Hale, 1989)

Warren-Clarke, L., *The Way of the Goddess* (Prism Press, 1987)

Wilson, C., *The Occult* (Granada, 1979)

— *Mysteries* (Granada, 1979)

York, M., 'New Age and Paganism', in Harvey and Hardman, (eds.), *Paganism Today* (Thorsons 1995) pp. 157–65.

Index